COOKING CUES
FROM
A TO Z

Roslyn Nemet

TIARA BOOKS   NEW YORK CITY

To Ava

My most beautiful cue

A TIARA COOKBOOK

Published by

Nordon Publications, Inc.
Two Park Avenue
New York, N.Y. 10016

A COOKBOOK

FOR THE WOMAN WHO ALREADY

HAS A COOKBOOK!

No matter how serious you are about cooking, you're bound to have at least one cookbook on your kitchen shelf, and probably more than one. But whether you're a gourmet chef who entertains frequently, a mother who cooks for her hungry family, or a businesswoman who dashes home from the the office just in time to toss a couple of chops in the pan, you'll find in COOKING CUES FROM A TO Z an indispensable aid to making the most of the time you spend in the kitchen.

It's the one volume the modern cook can't afford to be without!

We will send you a free catalog on request. Any titles not in your local bookstore can be purchased by mail. Send the price of the book plus 50¢ shipping charge to Tiara Books, P.O. Box 270, Norwalk, Connecticut 06852.

Titles currently in print are available for industrial and sales promotion at reduced rates. Address inquiries to Nordon Publications, Inc., Two Park Avenue, New York, New York 10016, Attention: Premium Sales Department.

INTRODUCTION

Did you ever find a really scrumptious-looking recipe which you were dying to try, only to discover that some of the terms used were unfamiliar to you? If a recipe tells you to *parboil*, do you know what to do? If pasta is to be cooked *al dente*, do you know what it means? If one of the ingredients is *kohlrabi*, do you know how to select it and what it tastes like?

Even the most experienced cook who is thoroughly at home with most culinary terms will sometimes find herself in a quandary and in need of a quick-and-easy reference work. COOKING CUES FROM A TO Z fills the bill. It deserves a prominent place on everyone's cookbook shelf, whether that shelf contains one dog-eared volume, or everything from the *Larousse Gastronomique* to Fanny Farmer. And the contents are arranged in alphabetical order so you don't waste precious time muddling through endless indexes in order to find the particular item you're looking for.

Aside from definitions and classifications, COOKING CUES FROM A TO Z also contains marketing tips, household hints, and short-cuts to make your cooking time more enjoyable, more productive, and easier.

AL DENTE: An Italian term used to describe food that is cooked firm to the bite, not overcooked.

ALMONDS: When buying unshelled almonds select those that are clean, free from cracks and are well filled so that the kernel does not rattle when shaken.

To blanch almonds, cover with boiling water and let stand for three minutes. Remove almonds from water, one at a time, slip off skins and let dry on paper towels for several hours.

To chop almonds, place in a blender, one-half cup at a time. Cover and whirl for thirty seconds at high speed.

The easiest way to grind almonds is to whirl them in a blender at high speed, one-quarter cup at a time. Watch very carefully or almonds will get pasty if over-whirled.

See also **NUTS.**

AMANDINE: A style of food prepared with a butter and sautéd almond sauce.

For a quick amandine sauce, sauté one-quarter cup blanched, shredded almonds in four tablespoons salted butter until lightly browned. Yields one-half cup.

AMBROSIA: A dessert consisting of orange slices and/or other fruits, sprinkled with sugar and shredded coconut.

For a zestier-looking ambrosia, use navel oranges for their brightness of color.

Try colored sugar instead of white for added sparkle and fun.

ANCHOVY: Belong to the herring family, narrow in shape and five to six inches long.

Anchovy fillets come in cans, either flat or rolled around a caper. Keep on hand for fast appetizers.

If anchovies are too salty, soak in cold water or milk for fifteen minutes; drain and pat dry.

Use anchovies to add zest to a plain sauce or a bland dish.

ANTIPASTO: One or several foods served in small quantities as a first course.

Antipasto may be arranged buffet style or on individual plates.

APPETIZERS: Small portions of hot or cold foods served either before a meal or as the first course of a meal. *See also* **CANAPES, HORS D'OEUVRES, COCKTAILS, DIPS, TIDBITS, RELISHES and SPREADS.**

APPLE: There are more than one-hundred varieties of apples. The most popular varieties for eating out of hand, in salads or appetizers are:

McIntosh—In season from October to February, slightly sweet and juicy.

Red Delicious—In season from September to April, mildly tart and juicy.

Golden Delicious—In season from October to April, sweet and juicy.

Baldwin—In season from November to April, mildly tart and juicy.

Those most suited for sauces and pies are:

Winesap—In season from January to May, slightly tart and juicy.

Stayman—In season from November to April, slightly tart and juicy.

Rhode Island Greening—In season from October to February, tart and juicy.

Rome Beauty—In season from November to May, mildly tart and juicy.

On the average, three apples equal one-pound.

Two-thirds of a pound equal two cups sliced.

One-pound equals two cups sauce.

When refrigerated, apples should be stored in plastic bags to prevent shriveling and transferring of odors.

To maintain shape when cooking, add sugar at *start* of cooking.

When cooking in sauces, add sugar *after* cooking.

A few apple slices placed in pan when cooking fish will hold down the fishy cooking odor.

A small apple, peeled and cut up, will deodorize refrigerator.

Add zest to apple dishes with a dash of nutmeg, cinnamon or allspice.

For chunky homemade applesauce, pare and core apples before cooking and beat only slightly with fork when they are done.

See also **FRUIT.**

APPLE PIE: For better taste, always serve apple pie warm.

Sprinkle the top crust of a store bought apple pie lightly with sugar and cinnamon before heating in the oven for a homemade taste and appearance.

One cup grated cheese sprinkled on the top crust adds zest to apple pie.

See also **PIE CRUST.**

APRICOTS: On the average, eight to ten apricots equal one-pound.

To ripen apricots, place in brown paper bag at room temperature. Ripe apricots will yield slightly to touch.

For easy peeling, dip fresh apricots in boiling and then cold water. Skins will slip right off.

Stored fresh apricots should be kept air tight to avoid aroma from mixing with other foods.

Dried apricots should be kept air tight to keep fruit moist.

For added flavor when cooking dried apricots, add one slice of lemon to each pound of apricots.

Drained, canned apricots filled with mint jelly make a beautiful and tasty garnish.

See also **FRUIT**.

ARROWROOT: A delicate thickening agent that is neutral in flavor. Produces soups, sauces, pie fillings and puddings that are clear and sparkling with none of the heaviness of other starches.

Easily digestible, suitable for invalid cookery.

ARTICHOKES: Purchase artichokes according to the way they are to be served. Select small size for pickling or stuffing; medium or large for salads; large for the hearts.

Artichokes should be thoroughly cleaned by soaking in cold, salted water for thirty minutes.

Thorny tip of each artichoke leaf should be trimmed off with scissors.

To avoid discoloration once artichokes are cut, place in mixture of three tablespoons of vinegar to one quart of water until cooking time.

Always drain artichokes upside down for fastest results.

For a different flavor, cook trimmed and drained artichokes in boiling chicken soup, covered, until tender. May be eaten hot, cold or in salad.

For easy eating, serve hot artichoke upright on a serving dish with individual dishes of melted butter. Pull off outer leaf, dip in melted butter, and enjoy!

For easy stuffed artichokes, cut off artichoke stems to one-half inch stubs. Cook in two inches boiling water in a deep covered saucepan until just barely tender, about thirty minutes. Pull off the tough outer leaves and discard. Snip off tips of remaining leaves with scissor and scoop out the prickly center with a spoon. Spread the leaves apart to form a cup. Fill with mixture of two tablespoons crab meat and one tablespoon buttered bread crumbs. Brush outside of artichoke with melted butter. Bake in a greased covered dish in a 350 degree oven for forty minutes. Uncover for ten minutes to brown tops.

Jerusalem artichokes may be dipped in any fritter batter and fried or just sliced and salted in any salad.

ASPARAGUS: One pound fresh asparagus usually serves three.

To eliminate sand and grit, wash under cold, running water, lifting and turning until clean.

For easiest results, use vegetable parer to shear off heavy scales.

Cut off stalks as far down as they will snap easily. White portion is usually tough.

To steam boil fresh asparagus, cook in a double boiler using the inverted top part of double boiler as the cover. The tough ends of the stalks should be placed down in the water and the tender tips up for steam cooking.

For tender, crisp results when sautéing or pan cooking asparagus, slice stalks slantwise approximately one-quarter inch thick.

See also **VEGETABLES.**

ASPIC: A clear jelly used to decorate and mold entrees, salads and canapes of meat, fish, poultry or eggs.

To easily unmold an aspic, brush mold lightly with oil before filling.

Season aspics more sharply by adding a little sherry, burgundy or brandy before molding.

Use chicken broth as the liquid when preparing a vegetable or chicken aspic.

For added color, add chopped pimientos and/or green peppers to aspic before jelling.

AU GRATIN: A cooking process which produces dishes with a crisp, cheesey, golden brown crust. Main ingredient has been moistened with possibly eggs or milk, then covered with bread crumbs and butter or cheese, finally baked or broiled.

AVOCADO: Select solid avocados with well developed neck or stem ends. Avoid those with dark soft spots, bruises and soft skins.

To ripen, keep at room temperature until soft to the touch.

A firm avocado is at the perfect stage to use as half-shell appetizers.

To remove pit, cut avocado in half and whack it with the flat side of a knife.

Medium soft avocados have a smooth eating texture and a mellow nutty flavor, excellent in combination with salads and vegetables.

Very soft avocados are perfect for all dishes that call for mashed or pureed fruit, as in dips, soups and dressings.

Always use stainless steel utensils when cutting or mashing avocados to avoid darkening and a metallic taste.

To avoid discoloration after avocado is sliced, sprinkle with lemon juice.

For peak taste, refrigerate avocado an hour or two before serving.

Avocado balls make a fancy garnish in salads. Scoop out balls with a melon cutter, sprinkle with lemon juice and toss in salad.

To grow your own avocado house plant, prop the pit on the rim of a glass of water with three toothpicks until roots form. Then transfer into soil, water frequently and watch a beautiful leafy plant grow before your eyes.

BABA AU RHUM: A glazed rum cake containing currants, raisins or candied fruits.

BACON: One pound package of bacon contains an average of sixteen to twenty slices.

When cooking bacon, do not permit bacon fat to smoke. This gives bacon a burned flavor.

For crisper bacon, drain off fat several times during cooking.

Canadian bacon is well cooked when the lean part is a red brown and the fat is a light golden brown.

For less shrinkage in bacon, bake in a 400 degree oven until crisp, turning once, instead of frying.

To prepare bacon in large quantities, place on a rack over a dripping pan in a 400 degree oven until crisp and brown.

Strain leftover bacon fat and use for sautéing eggs or potatoes and for seasoning vegetables.

Freeze small quantities of cooked bacon in foil for quick breakfast treats. Just heat and eat.

BAKE: To cook by dry heat, usually in an oven.

Always preheat oven before baking.

Always have ingredients at room temperature before baking.

Sift dry baking ingredients onto a paper plate, just blend for easy pouring.

How to test oven temperature without a thermometer; place a piece of white tissue paper on a baking pan in heated oven and:

Slow oven—tissue turns delicate brown in five minutes.
Moderate oven—tissue turns medium brown in five minutes.
Hot oven—tissue turns dark brown in five minutes.
Very hot oven—tissue turns very deep dark brown in three minutes.

BAKED ALASKA: An elegant dessert consisting of ice cream and cake with a meringue topping.

Never use sherbet when making Baked Alaska as it contains water and melts very quickly. Purchase the creamiest ice cream you can buy for best results.

To prevent melting of ice cream, be certain that ice cream is hard and completely covered by meringue before baking. The air in the meringue acts as an insulator and prevents heat from penetrating to ice cream.

17

For added zest, sprinkle shredded coconut on meringue before baking.

BAKING POWDER: To test for freshness, stir a small amount of baking powder into a little water. If it bubbles, it's active and may be used.

BAKING SODA: To test for freshness, stir a small amount of baking soda into lemon juice or vinegar. If it bubbles, it's active and may be used.

BANANAS: Select yellow-colored skin with brown flecks for eating; slightly green for cooking.

Bananas may be kept in refrigerator to prevent further ripening. Skins will turn dark but bananas will remain white.

To prevent darkening when peeled, sprinkle with any citrus juice.

BARBECUE: Foods cooked over an open fire; over coals; in a pit; or on a spit in front of a fire.

Use charcoal briquettes for an even, intense fire.

Start fire forty-five minutes before actual cooking for correct temperature.

Meats should be marinated or brushed with a barbecue sauce before or during cooking to prevent dryness.

Use long insulated gloves and barbecue tools with long handles for easy, carefree barbecuing.

In case of fire, keep sand handy to control blaze if it should flare up when drippings fall.

For an unexpected delight, skewer scallops and toast as you would marshmallows. Then just dip in cold tartar sauce and eat immediately.

Use heat remaining in coals after main meal is cooked to toast marshmallows for a fun dessert.

BASIL: Herb with clovelike flavor. Sweet and mildly pungent.

Traditionally used on tomatoes, cooked or raw in salads.

Tasty with lamb chops, cheese dishes, and such vegetables as peas and string beans.

See also **HERBS & SPICES.**

BASTE: To brush or pour liquid over meat or other food while it is cooking.

BATTER: A mixture of flour, liquid and other ingredients to cook as is or to be used as an outer coating for frying.

Do not overbeat batters as this will cause batter to be tough.

For a more successful batter, permit it to stand a few minutes before using. Ingredients will have time to set and will then coat food better.

To assure that batter will adhere to food, be certain food is completely dry before coating.

BEANS: *Green or wax beans* should be of medium size and crisp enough to snap easily.

Try serving them topped with sour cream for a different and delicious flavor.

Lima beans should have clean, well-filled dark green pods.

Shell them just before cooking by cutting pods open with a scissor.

A general rule for cooking beans is to add one-half teaspoon salt per pound of beans to the boiling water.

See also **VEGETABLES and DRIED BEANS.**

BEAT: To whip with a spoon or beater so that ingredients are combined and air is introduced into mixture.

BEEF: Beef is an important element in our diet and is often a major factor in the planning of nutritious meals for the family. It ranks as high in nutrition as it does in popularity.

Beef of excellent quality is recognized by its bright red, fine-grained texture and is liberally marbled with fat which is white in color rather than yellow.

Beef grades are:
Prime—the top quality beef.

Choice—almost as juicy as prime but has less fat.
Good—usually has little fat and is less succulent.
Commercial and Utility—beef from older animals which requires long, slow cooking.

To prevent bacterial growth and dryness, beef should be defrosted in the refrigerator while still in its wrappings.

Beef roasts should be completely defrosted before cooking or the center may be scarcely warmed when the outside is thoroughly done.

Beef should be removed from refrigerator one hour before cooking so that it cooks evenly.

Do not wash meat before cooking or valuable juices will be lost. Just wipe with a cold, damp cloth.

Retain meat juices by salting meat *after* it is cooked.

Less expensive cuts of meat boast the same nutritional value as higher priced steaks or roasts. The secret is slow cooking for tender results.

Beef rule of thumb serving portions are:

	Servings per pound[1]
Much bone or gristle........................	1 or 2
Medium amounts of bone....................	2 or 3
Little or no bone............................	3 or 4

[1]Three ounces of cooked lean meat per serving.

Pounding and marinating are two methods used to tenderize meat.

Marinades serve two purposes; firstly for tenderizing and secondly for flavoring. Packaged marinades are fast and easy, just add liquid.

A beef roast should be placed in pan with the fat side up to eliminate basting.

Always remember roasts continue to cook for about five minutes after removal from the oven.

Timetable for roasting:

Kind and cut of meat	Ready-to-cook weight	Approximate roasting time at 325° F.	Internal temperature of meat when done
Standing ribs:	Pounds	Hours	°F.
Rare...............	6 to 8	2 1/2 to 3	140
Medium..........	6 to 8	3 to 3 1/2	160
Well done........	6 to 8	3 2/3 to 5	170
Rolled rump:			
Rare............	5	2 1/4	140
Medium..........	5	3	160
Well done........	5	3 1/4	170
Sirloin tip:			
Rare............	3	1 1/2	140
Medium..........	3	2	160
Well done........	3	2 1/4	170

Timetable for braising:

Kind and cut of meat	Approximate ready-to-cook weight or thickness	Approximate total cooking time
Pot roast, such as chuck or round	3 to 5 pounds	3 to 4
Steak, such as chuck or round	1 to 1 1/2 inches	2 to 2 1/2
Short ribs	2 to 2 1/2 pounds	2 to 2 1/2

For better results, select a thick steak for cooking rare and a thin one for cooking well done.

Before broiling, slash fat around edge of steak to prevent curling.

Never use a fork when turning steaks as piercing permits the juices to escape. Use tongs.

A tough steak can be tenderized by brushing both sides with a mixture of 1 tablespoon vinegar and 2 tablespoons oil or butter. Let stand several hours before using.

Never permit a stew to boil as it will toughen and shrivel the meat. Simmer very slowly over a low heat.

When shaping balls, burgers or loaves of ground meat, use a light touch. Too much handling will result in hard, juiceless meat.

When shaping ground beef, dip your fingers in water to prevent sticking.

For normal tastes, one pound of ground beef requires three-quarters teaspoon salt.

For juicier burgers, add a grated potato to each pound of ground meat.

Timetable for Broiling:

Kind and cut of meat	Approximate thickness	Degree of doneness	Approximate total cooking time[1]
	Inches		Minutes
Beef steaks..........	1	Rare........	10 to 15
(Club, porterhouse,	1	Medium	15 to 20
rib, sirloin, T-bone,	1	Well done...	20 to 30
tenderloin)........	1 1/2	Rare........	15 to 20
	1 1/2	Medium	20 to 25
	1 1/2	Well done...	25 to 40
	2	Rare........	25 to 35
	2	Medium	35 to 45
	2	Well done...	45 to 55
Hamburgers.........	3/4	Rare........	8
	3/4	Medium	12
	3/4	Well done...	14

[1]Meat at refrigerator temperature at start of broiling.

When frying burgers, sprinkle the bottom of a preheated pan lightly with salt. Meat will then fry in its own juices and form a crispy crust.

Properly prepared fried meats are crisp on the outside and moist on the inside.

For even frying, meat should be of uniform size and of room temperature.

Meat should be well dried before frying to avoid fat from spattering.

When frying, level of oil should be three inches below top of pan to permit room for bubbling.

Never overcrowd pan. Fry a few pieces at a time.

Strain fat through several layers of cheese cloth and use again for frying similar foods. May then be stored in refrigerator.

BEETS: Select beets with fresh, young-looking leaves. Small and medium sized beets are usually the most tender.

Beet greens may be prepared and eaten like spinach.

A few caraway seeds added to any beet recipe will add zest.

See also **VEGETABLES.**

BISQUE: A thick cream soup usually made from fish.

A frozen dessert or ice cream made with crushed macaroons.

BLANCH: To parboil or to pour boiling water over a food; then drain and rinse with cold water.

Mainly used to remove skins from nuts.

Blanching is used to shrink vegetables and fruits for canning and freezing.

BLEND: To mix two or more ingredients thoroughly.

BLUEBERRIES: Select berries that are bright blue with a slightly frosted look for peak taste.

Wash berries carefully and remove all bits of leaf and stem before serving.

Fresh blueberries may be frozen as is in air tight containers.

For a delicious easy dessert, combine confectioners suger with ginger to taste; sprinkle on top of ice cold blueberries.

Interchangeable in any recipe calling for huckle-berries.

BOIL: To cook in liquid in which bubbles constantly rise to the surface and break.

BORSCH: A delicious beet soup, generally served cold.

The trick when making borsch is to use enough lemon juice. After the meat is tender, add additional juice of one-half lemon to any borsch recipe. Then continue cooking fifteen minutes longer.

BOUILLABAISSE: A fish and soup dish.

For the very best bouillabaisse, add a pinch of saffron.

Always serve the fish and soup in separate dishes but at the same time.

For easy serving, prepare two hot serving dishes. Then strain the soup into one and place the fish in the other.

Always serve toast with bouillabaisse, the expected accompaniment.

BOUQUET GARNI: An assortment of herbs and spices.

To make a Bouquet Garni, wrap dried herbs in 4-inch squares of heavy cheesecloth. Include a bay leaf and one-half teaspoon each of thyme, parsley, basil, marjoram, savory and chervil. Gather the four corners of the cheesecloth together and tie them securely.

These bouquets of dried ingredients may be made in advance and stored in tightly covered containers, away from light.

Use in soups and stews. Add to the last one-half hour of cooking and remove before serving.

Never use a bouquet more than once.

BRAISE: A method of cooking wherein food is first browned in a small amount of fat in an open pan. It is then cooked further over low heat, tightly covered, with small amount of liquid added, if desired.

This is the best method for cooking less tender cuts of meat

BRAZIL NUTS: To shell easily, cover nuts with boiling water and boil for three minutes. Drain; cool and shell.

To slice without breaking, cover with cold water and slowly bring to a boil. Simmer three minutes; drain and slice.

See also **NUTS.**

BREAD: To freshen bread, place in a wet paper bag. Fasten the bag tightly and place in a 350 degree oven until bag is dry (10 to 20 minutes).

To slice reheated bread, cut with a hot knife. Dip blade in hot water to heat.

Keep bread and cake in different tin containers as cake will draw moisture from bread.

BREAD CRUMBS: For easy, homemade bread

crumbs, cut stale bread into pieces and place in a 250 degree oven until crisp. Then grind in blender.

BREAD PUDDING: For a tastier homemade bread pudding, try toasting bread first and then buttering it before using in your usual recipe.

BROCCOLI: Select dark green heads with tightly closed buds. Yellowish leaves indicate poor quality.

To thoroughly clean, soak in salted water to remove insects and chemical dust.

For even cooking, make lengthwise gashes starting at the ends of the stalks to insure softness as the floweret tops will cook faster.

To preserve the green color, add a teaspoon of lemon juice to the boiling water when cooking.

To cut down odor when cooking, toss a heel of bread on top before covering the pot. Remove after cooking.

See also **VEGETABLES.**

BROIL: To cook directly under or above a source of radiant heat which may be gas, electric, charcoal, or an open fire.

BROILER: A young, tender chicken, weighing from 3/4 to 3 1/2 pounds, used for broiling and frying.

See also **POULTRY.**

BROWN SUGAR: To soften brown sugar that is caked and lumpy, place in a baking dish and bake in a 200 degree oven for ten minutes or until soft. Then roll with a rolling pin until all lumps disappear.

To keep moist and soft, refrigerate before opening and keep tightly closed package in refrigerator between use.

One pound firmly packed brown sugar yields 2 1/4 cups.

BRUSSEL SPROUTS: Select fresh, green, compact heads; loose heads are an indication of poor quality.

One pound usually serves four.

To thoroughly clean, soak in salted water for thirty minutes to remove insects and chemical dust.

For even cooking, cut small gashes lengthwise across stems to ensure softness. Heads cook faster than stems.

See also **VEGETABLES.**

BUFFET: A meal where guests help themselves from a table on which the foods are placed in a decorative and appetizing manner.

BUTTER: To prevent butter from burning when sautéeing, add a little salad or olive oil.

To *clarify* butter, melt butter in a small pan over low heat. When it is melted, carefully pour off the clear butter and discard any sediment or milk left in pan.

BUTTERMILK: Milk that is left after butter has been churned.

To substitute buttermilk for fresh milk in a recipe, use baking soda instead of baking powder for leavening.

Example: one-half cup buttermilk plus one-quarter teaspoon baking soda will equal one-half cup fresh milk plus one teaspoon baking powder.

BUTTERNUTS: To shell easily, pour boiling water over nuts and let stand for fifteen minutes. Then drain and shell.

See also **NUTS.**

CABBAGE: Select solid heads which are heavy for their size. Avoid heads showing yellow leaves, a sign of age and poor quality.

One pound of cabbage yields 3 1/2 cups raw or 2 1/2 cups cooked.

For easy cole slaw so that dressing may soak into cabbage more rapidly, cabbage should be coarsely grated.

To preserve color when cooking red cabbage, add one teaspoon of lemon juice or a few slices of a fresh apple.

To cut down odor when cooking cabbage, toss a heel of bread on top before covering the pot. Remove after cooking.

See also **VEGETABLES.**

CAKES: For quick, delicious cakes, start with a packaged mix but substitute fruit juice for the water indicated in package directions.

Any cake mix can be given a homemade taste and touch by adding grated chocolate, nutmeats or coconut.

Fillings in cakes will hold better if cake layers are placed wth bottoms together.

To avoid fall-in, spongecakes should be immmediately inverted upon removal from oven.

When preparing chocolate cakes, dust pan with cocoa instead of flour before baking.

To prevent chocolate chips from sinking to the bottom of cakes, dust chips before adding to batter. Use cocoa for chocolate cakes and flour for all other flavors.

If cake sticks to bottom of pan when removing, place a cloth of hot water under pan until cake loosens.

Measure and follow directions carefully because:

Too much flour—cake is dry and crumbly.
Too much fat—cake is oily and may fall.
Too much sugar—cake will be sticky or have hard crust.
Too much liquid—cake will fall easily.
Too much soda—cake has bad color and disagreeable taste.
Too much kneading—prevents rising.

To make store bought fruitcake seem homemade, sprinkle with brandy every few days for a couple of weeks.

Rich fruitcake improves in flavor if aged at least two weeks before using.

Homemade frosting gives a plain store bought cake that homemade taste.

Simple icing may be made by just melting butter-scotch or chocolate chips in a double boiler

CANAPES: Small hot or cold appetizers served on cut bread which has been trimmed free of crust.

Cookie cutters may be used for an assortment of interesting bread shapes.

Melba toast and crackers may also be used as a base for canapes.

CANTALOUPE: Select melons with a fruity fragrance and which are slightly soft to the touch, a sign of ripeness.

Ripen melons at room temperature; do not refrigerate until then.

For a fast and easy dessert, serve cantaloupe halves filled with ice cream or assorted fruit.

Cantaloupe balls make a beautiful garnish and add zest to any dish. For best results, cut melon with a melon scooper.

CAPERS: The unopened flowers of the caper bush. Buds are picked before petals can expand and preserved in vinegar and salt.

Capers add zest to sauces, salads, creamed dishes and as condiments to meats and seafood.

CAPON: Male chickens which have been castrated at six to eight weeks of age to produce birds with more tender flesh and a generous fat covering. Weight 4 to 8 pounds, used for roasting.

See also **POULTRY.**

CARAFE: An ornamental glass water bottle for table use.

CARAMELIZE: To heat sugar or food containing sugar until a brown color and characteristic flavor develops.

To caramelize sugar, heat sugar in a heavy saucepan, stirring constantly, until a golden brown syrup is formed. Remove from heat immediately.

To caramelize a mold is to coat it with sugar in the caramelized stage.

CARP: A fresh water fish of the minnow family.

Select carp with pink gills, tight shiny scales and a bright looking skin with firm flesh.

Skinning carp and soaking it in mild salt water helps remove its muddy flavor.

Very perishable. Cleaned and dressed fish should be

wrapped in moisture proof paper and refrigerated immediately. Cook as soon as possible.

See also **FISH.**

CARROTS: Select young thin carrots with fresh green tops for sweetness and peak flavor.

One pound serves three or four.

Scrub young carrots with a stiff brush. Do not peel, valuable vitamins will be preserved by using this method.

Scrape older, larger carrots with a potato peeler for easier handling.

See also **VEGETABLES.**

CASSEROLE: A cooked meal in which a number of ingredients are simmered together either in the oven or on top of the stove.

CASSEROLE DISH: A deep cooking vessel designed to retain heat and to be used for long, slow cooking.

CAULIFLOWER: Select heads that are compact, white or creamy white with clean flowerets and bright green leaves.

A medium size head serves four.

Before cooking or serving, soak in salted water to remove chemical dust.

Cauliflower flowerets may be served raw in salads or as an accompaniment to dips.

To prevent cauliflower from darkening, add one teaspoon of vinegar to water before cooking.

To cut down odor when cooking, toss a heel of bread on top before covering pot. Remove after cooking.

See also **VEGETABLES.**

CELERY: For peak flavor, select crisp, firm stalks with fresh leaves that snap easily.

Remove celery leaves and save for future use in soups and salads.

Use outer stalks for cooking and more tender inner stalks for eating raw.

Save small tender celery hearts to use as a relish or in salads.

To revive slightly wilted celery, place in a bowl of ice water for a short time.

To make celery very crisp, add one teaspoon of sugar to a quart of ice water and marinate celery in it for thirty minutes.

See also **VEGETABLES.**

CHAFING DISH: A vessel for cooking at the table and for keeping foods hot (for buffet use).

CHARCOAL BROILER: For best results, light broiler and let it warm up completely before using.

Before cooking, grates should be cleaned and scraped of charcoal residue with a stiff wire brush.

To prevent meat from sticking, lubricate the grates by rubbing the fat part of the meat across the surface before cooking.

To prevent juices from escaping, use tongs when turning food.

CHATEAUBRIAND: Filet of beef cut on the diagonal from the thickest part of the tenderloin. Weighs from 1 to 1 1/4 pounds and generally serves two.

CHEESE: Cheese was made and eaten in Biblical times. Like its classic cohorts, bread and wine, it is made by the process of fermentation.

Nutritively speaking, cheese is a nearly perfect food. It contains essential food elements the body needs such as proteins, fats and vitamins.

All cheese falls into two categories; natural or processed.

Natural cheese is cured in many different ways to produce a variety of soft-creamy-hard-strong-mild-odorous-or tangy flavors and textures.
Processed cheese is made by grinding and blending natural cheese and heating it with an emulsifying salt.

Cheese goes well with almost every course and is ideal for in-between meal snacks.

When hard cheese becomes too dry, wrap a cloth dampened with warm water around it. The heat and moisture will soften the cheese.

Mold which developes on cheese is not harmful. Merely scrape it off and use the remaining cheese.

When cooking with cheese, heat at a low temperature. Cooking too fast or too long makes cheese tough or stringy.

When cooking with cheese on top of stove, be sure to use a double boiler to prevent scorching.

To melt dried out grated cheese in cooking, add a little milk.

The best grating cheeses are hard and dry; cheddar, gruyer, parmesan, romano.

Always use a fine grater for shredding hard cheese and a coarse grater for shredding soft cheese.

Processed cheese melts at a lower temperature than natural cheese and makes a smoother sauce.

The one universal rule for cheese is it should be removed from refrigerator and kept at room temperature for two hours to mellow before serving. Of course, the exception to this rule is cottage, ricotta and cream cheese.

After cheese has been opened, the rule of thumb is to keep air out and moisture in. Place in a dome before serving.

Strong cheese should be wrapped securely and then stored in a tightly covered container in refrigerator to prevent other foods from picking up their odor.

Only certain natural cheeses may be frozen in small quantities, one pound or less: Edam, Gouda, Swiss, Meunster, Provolone. Mozzarella, Cheddar and Brick.

Always thaw frozen cheese in the refrigerator and use as soon as possible.

Mild cheddar may be substituted for Jack cheese.

Grated Romano and Parmesan cheese may be substituted for grated Cheddar.

Cottage cheese may be substituted for Ricotta. However, Ricotta has a higher fat content and is creamier than Cottage cheese. It also has a less piquant flavor. Texture of recipe will be slightly changed with this substitution.

Stilton, Blue and Roquefort cheeses are very similar in appearance and consistency. Blue and Stilton are both made from whole cow's milk but Stilton has cream added. Roquefort is made from sheep's milk and has more of a tendency to crumble. All may be used interchangeably.

Pot cheese may be substituted for Cottage cheese. Cottage cheese is made from skim milk with cream and salt added while Pot cheese has neither cream nor salt. Texture of recipe will not be altered by use of either cheese.

Instead of dressing, try adding a grating of cheese to a salad.

CHERRIES: Select large dark Bing cherries that are firm, meaty and smooth-skinned for peak flavor.

To remove pits from cherries (for fruit salad), insert a new pen point into a pen holder with the pointed end in. You will then have a scoop perfect in size for removing pits.

Pitted cherries (fresh or canned) stuffed with whole nut meats make a delicious garnish or in a fruit salad.

See also **FRUIT.**

CHERVIL: Has a mild, parsleylike flavor and a delightful aroma.

For better flavor, chervil should be chopped.

Use as a garnish to top cream soups and salads, egg dishes and fish.

See also **HERBS & SPICES.**

CHESTNUTS: Select chestnuts which are plump and free from blemishes or cracks.

One pound yields about 2 1/2 cups shelled and peeled nuts.

Before cooking, always slash the flat side of each nut with a sharp knife.

Keep cooked, peeled chestnuts in warm water until ready to peel or the inner skin will not come off.

See also **NUTS.**

CHICKEN: *See* **POULTRY.**

CHIVES: Akin to the onion but more delicate in taste.

Use chives to flavor any food in which a mild onion flavor is desired.

For peak flavor, chives should be cut and added to foods just before serving.

Chives make a zesty garnish for boiled potatoes, cottage cheese and all salads.

See also **HERBS & SPICES.**

CHOP: To cut coarsely with a knife or cleaver.

CHOWDER: A thick, hearty soup containing either fish or seafood, salt pork, vegetables and milk. Other varieties are all vegetable or vegetables combined with meat. The most popular chowders are New England Clam Chowder and Manhattan Clam Chowder.

CHUTNEY: A seasoned relish made from a mixture of chopped fruits and spices.

CINNAMON: A spice used extensively in cookies, cakes and with fruits.

See also **HERBS & SPICES.**

CLAMS: Do not purchase clams with broken shells or shells that are slightly open, a sign of poor quality.

For thorough cleaning, clams should be scrubbed with a stiff brush before opening.

Quick, gentle cooking will keep clams from toughening.

The smaller clams are known as littlenecks. Medium clams are known as cherry stones. Both are suited for eating raw.

Larger clams have a stronger flavor and are best suited for chowders.

When preparing steamers (may be either little-necks or cherry stones), use one quart unshucked steamers per person.

CLARIFY: To separate the solid parts of fat from the liquid parts. To make pure and clear.

Liquids are clarified by filtering whereas fats are clarified by slow heating.

For example see Butter.

CLOVES: The dried flower buds from the clove tree which have a spicy taste.

Stud a ham with cloves for better taste and appearance before baking.

A clove studded onion adds zest to soups, creamed dishes and sauces. Remove onion and cloves before serving.

A clove studded orange makes a delightful freshener when placed in a clothes closet.

See also **HERBS & SPICES.**

COCKTAILS: Cocktails are a form of appetizer served at the table with a sauce or dressing.

Cocktails should always be served ice cold.

Seafood and fruit are those most frequently used—shrimp cocktail being among the most popular.

COCOA: To preserve freshness, store dry cocoa in airtight container in a cool place.

When serving hot cocoa, use a cinnamon stick as a stirrer for added zest.

For frothy hot cocoa, beat before serving.

For enriched hot cocoa, add three tablespoons of dry milk for each cupful of liquid.

COCONUT: Select those coconuts which are heavy for their size and sound full of liquid when shaken.

1 medium coconut yields three to four cups of grated coconut and almost one cup of milk.

To shell, pierce two of the three eyes at the end of the coconut and drain off the liquid. Heat coconut in a 350 degree oven for twenty to thirty minutes. Tap coconut all over with a hammer and then it will be easy to break open. Pare the inner brown skin off with a knife and pry out white meat.

To grate white meat easiest, whirl in a blender.

To renew softness of coconut, heat over hot water.

COCOTTE DISH: Small china or earthenware dish with 'ears' on each side or with one handle, 1 1/2 inches deep.

Used to bake and serve eggs.

COFFEE: To preserve freshness, opened coffee should be stored in refrigerator.

To preserve freshness, instant coffee should be stored in freezer for that just-opened flavor.

One cup of brewed coffee added to stews adds color, taste and zest.

Freeze cubes with instant coffee for use in iced coffee drinks.

COLANDER: A vessel with perforated sides and bottom, used in draining off liquids in cookery (a non-flexible strainer).

COLESLAW: Uncooked, shredded green or red cabbage, combined with other ingredients and dressing.

For wilted coleslaw, mix shredded cabbage mixture with dressing immediately and let stand in refrigerator until ready to serve.

For crisp coleslaw, place shredded cabbage mixture in refrigerator until ready to serve and *then* mix in dressing.

COLLARDS: Belong to the cabbage family and are most closely related to kale.

Select fresh, young, tender leaves that are free from blemishes and seed stems.

Must be washed thoroughly in cold water to remove sand.

When cooking, remove tough stems and midribs of leaves. Cut large leaves into pieces.

Also used as a salad green. See SALADS.

COMPOTE: Fresh, canned or dried fruits that have been cooked and served in their own juices. May be served hot or cold.

CONFECTIONERS SUGAR: Granulated sugar that has been crushed very fine and mixed with cornstarch to prevent caking.

Used for frostings, confections, sauces and dusting of pastries.

CONVECTION OVEN: A method of cooking foods by recirculating a stream of heated air which cooks foods from thirty to fifty percent faster than conventional methods.

Uses about half the amount of gas as the standard pilot type gas range.

High-speed, hot-air currents start to cook food *immediately* resulting in a saving of time and energy.

Cooks frozen meats from the freezer in approximately the same time as thawed meats in a conventional oven.

COOKIES: Avoid the use of too much flour when rolling out cookie dough. Try a little confectioners sugar instead for better flavor.

To make neat uniform indentations in thumb-print type cookies, try a lightly floured cork saved from a whisky bottle.

As a general cue, bake cookies until delicately brown and firm at the edge.

To test for doneness of dark-colored cookies (chocolate or ginger), look for a dry surface and firm edges.

For cookies that have been spread in pan for cutting after baking, watch for dough to shrink from the edges. It should also be done if the top springs back after you lightly press it.

To keep cookies from drying out, put a section of an apple in the cookie jar.

CORN: For freshness, select corn with bright green snug husks and dark brown silk at husk end.

For easy removal of silk between kernel rows, brush with a dry vegetable brush.

Two ears of corn yield one and a third cups of kernels.

Cook corn as soon as possible. Texture, flavor and half of the sugar content is lost in the first twenty-four hours after being picked.

Never cook corn in salted water, the kernels toughen. Salt after cooking.

For easy buttering of corn for a crowd, melt one tablespoon of butter or margarine for each ear of corn in a long shallow pan. Add salt and pepper. Then roll cooked corn in pan until each ear is well coated.

See also **VEGETABLES.**

CORNMEAL: Refrigerate to maintain freshness.

To prevent from lumping, wet thoroughly with cold water before pouring in the boiling water.

CORNSTARCH: Used as a thickener in sauces, gravies and puddings. When used in baking cakes, it ensures "keeping quality" and makes cake easier to slice.

CRANBERRY: Select fresh cranberries that are firm and plump with a high luster which indicates ripeness.

One pound of fresh cranberries yields four cups of sauce.

Store cranberries in refrigerator unwashed and covered until ready to use. Moisture hastens spoilage.

CREAM: The process of working one or more foods until they are soft and creamy.

CREAM OF TARTAR: A natural fruit acid in the form of a fine white powder made from pressed grapes.

An important ingredient in commercial baking powder.

For a creamier consistency in frostings, add a dash of cream of tartar.

For firmer egg whites, add a dash of cream of tartar before beating.

CRÊPE: A very thin egg batter pancake. The first step in making blintzes or flaming crêpes.

CRÊPE PAN: A thick, heavy based, shallow pan usually made of cast-iron, about six to seven inches in diameter. Makes crêpe cooking an absolute joy.

CROCK POT: See SLOW COOKER.

CROUTON: Small, cubed pieces of bread which have been fried in oil or butter or browned in the oven.

Generally used as a soup accompaniment but try tossing a few croutons in your salads.

CRUET: Small glass bottle to contain seasonings, oil or vinegar at table.

CUBE: To cut into small, even pieces.

CUCUMBER: Select firm, dark green, slender cucumbers for best quality.

One medium size cucumber yields 1 1/2 cups diced.

For easy peeling, scrape with a potato peeler.

For easy removal of wax on the skins of cucumbers, brush with a vegetable brush.

To preserve vitamins and freshness, peel or slice cucumbers just before using.

CURE: A method of preserving meat, poultry or vegetables using salt as the preservative.

Saltpeter is added to preserve and intensify red color.

Sugar is sometimes added for flavor.

Pork is the most frequently cured meat.

CURRANTS: Fresh, tiny, sweet-tart berries which come in red, white or black.

Fresh *red* currants are eaten as is or cooked in jams and jellies.

Fresh *white* currants are used in salads and fruit cups.

Fresh *black* currants are used primarily in jams, jellies and beverages.

Dried currants are actually tiny, black, seedless grapes which are used primarily in cakes and cookies. They are tarter and more highly flavored than raisins.

Five ounces of dried currants equals one cup.

CUSTARD: A mixture of eggs and milk, sweetened, flavored and cooked over hot water on top of stove or set in a pan of hot water and baked in oven.

For perfect custards, avoid overbeating. Stir only to blend; do not make a froth.

Always place dish containing custard in a pan of pre-heated hot water while baking.

For enriched custard, add three tablespoons of dry milk to each cupful of liquid.

DATES: For easy cutting, use scissors dipped frequently in cold water.

For extra taste, add cut-up dates to fruit cups or salads.

DECANT: To pour gently so as not to stir up the dregs.

DECANTER: A vessel used to hold decanted liquors.

DEEP FRY: To fry food in fat which is deep enough to cover it completely.

DELMONICO: A famous restaurant noted for certain outstanding dishes, especially a cut of beef known as a Delmonico steak.

DEMITASSE: A small cup of black coffee usually served after dinner.

DESSERT: The closing course of a meal.

Desserts may run the gamut, from the simplest to the most elegant, depending upon your mood but it is always best to select a dessert that enhances your menu.

If you are planning a heavy meal, serve a light dessert; for a light meal serve a rich dessert.

Sweets of every description, fruits, pastries, are all appropriate desserts.

DEVILED: Foods that have been highly seasoned with spices and other condiments.

DEVIL'S FOOD: A rich, dark and yummy chocolate cake.

DEVONSHIRE CREAM: A delicious rich sauce made from non-homogenized fresh farm milk into a thick, clotted cream.

DICE: To cut into cubes, usually one-quarter-inch long, with a sharp knife.

DILL: An aromatic herb used for flavoring soups, sauces and particularly pickles.

Dill seeds and leaves have a faint caraway tang.

Chopped fresh dill adds zest to French dressing.

Tasty on cole slaw, macaroni and a sauce for broiled fish of all kinds.

See also **HERBS & SPICES.**

DIPS: Mixtures soft enough to be scooped up with crackers, chips or crisp vegetables but firm enough so that they will not drip off the scoopers.

For a nice change, serve a dip in a scooped-out red cabbage or avocado.

DISSOLVE: To liquefy a solid food, to melt.

DIVINITY: A creamy candy, made with sugar, water, corn syrup and stiffly beaten egg whites.

DOT: To place small amounts of an ingredient over the top surface of food.

DOUBLE BOILER: A very useful cooking utensil. One covered pan fits inside another pan in a hot water bath. This allows slow cooking, with no fear of burning, and prevents the curdling of custards and sauces.

DOUGH: To test yeast dough, press two fingers into the dough. The depression made by the fingers will fill quickly if dough is not ready. If holes remain, it has risen enough.

Avoid the overuse of flour when rolling cookie dough. For a better flavor, try powdered sugar instead.

DOUGHNUTS: A small ring of cake dough that has been deep fried to a golden brown.

For less greasy doughnuts, let stand for about fifteen minutes before frying. Rested doughnuts absorb less fat.

For easier handling, use chopsticks to turn.

DREDGE: To sprinkle a food with a dry substance such as flour, cornmeal, fine bread crumbs or sugar.

DRESSING: A sauce, usually cold, added to fish, meats, fruits and most usually to salads.

A solid, well-seasoned mixture used to stuff fish, poultry or meats; or can be baked by itself (stuffing).

A method of preparing food for cooking. Poultry is dressed by plucking, drawing, singeing, trimming and trussing. Fish is dressed by scaling, gutting and trimming.

DRIED BEANS: Dried beans require soaking. Use 2 1/2 cups water for 1 cup of blackeye beans (blackeye peas, cowpeas) Great Northern beans, and lima beans. Use 3 cups water for 1 cup of kidney beans, pea (navy) beans, and pinto beans.

To soak beans quickly, boil two minutes, remove from heat and let stand one hour.

For better tasting beans, cook in the soaking water, add one teaspoon salt for each cup of beans and boil gently for the time given below:

Blackeye	one-half hour
Great Northern	one to one-and-one-half hours
Kidney	two hours
Lentils	as recipe indicates
Lima	one hour
Pea	one-and-one-half to two hours
Pinto	two hours

It should be noted that packaged lentils may or may not require soaking. Follow box instructions carefully.

To properly cook lentils, drop in rapidly boiling water slowly so as not to disturb the boiling point. Then lower heat to simmer until lentils are tender.

Due to their blandness, lentils require high seasoning.

When using lentils in soup, cook until they mash easily.

To cook beans more quickly, add one-eighth teaspoon baking soda to water for each cup of dried beans. Reduces cooking time about 25%.

To reduce foaming when cooking, add one tablespoon of fat for each cup of beans to the cooking water.

If acid ingredients like tomatoes, ketchup or vinegar are included in the recipe, add them after the beans are tender. Acid prevents softening of beans.

DRIED FRUIT: Large portion of water content in fresh fruit has been evaporated.

Delicious when used for compotes.

DRIP: A steady flow of liquid, drop by drop.

DRIPPINGS: Fat or juice that is drawn from food during cooking.

Fat from drippings can be used as shortening in making gravies, sauces, piecrust, biscuits and breads.

DUCK: When purchasing, allow one pound uncooked duck per person.

Small ducks are suitable for broiling or frying; larger ones for roasting or rotisserie cooking.

It is not necessary to truss ducks due to short legs and wings.

Before roasting, prick duck well in several places so that fat can drain off. Pour off fat as it accumulates to prevent spattering in oven.

For added color and crisper skin, increase the oven temperature to 425 degrees for the last ten minutes of roasting time.

Doneness can be tested by pressing drumstick meat between protected fingers.

Apricot flavor enhances all duck dishes.

As a rule of thumb, sharp spices and dry stuffings are tastiest with ducks.

See also **POULTRY.**

DUMPLING: A small amount of dough, shaped into a ball, and cooked by broiling or steaming.

Use a large pot to allow for swelling of dumplings during cooking.

For better tasting dumplings, cook in liquid that just simmers rather than a fast boil.

For fluffier dumplings, cook uncovered until dumplings rise to the surface, then cover pot until done.

DUST: To sprinkle lightly with flour or sugar.

DUTCH OVEN: A heavy-bottomed deep pot with a tight fitting convex lid.

DUXELLES: Dry cooked mushrooms used as a flavoring in French cooking.

ECLAIRS: An oblong pastry puff filled with custard or whipped cream and topped with a thin chocolate icing.

For perfect shaping, use a pastry bag and tube. Eclairs should be finger-shaped oblongs, 1 x 4 1/2 inches.

For a change, try miniatures, 3/4 x 2 inches long.

EGGNOG: The flavor of eggnog depends upon quality ingredients. Use the freshest eggs, the heaviest cream, and the finest brandy and rum you can afford.

The most important cue for eggnog is to serve it ice cold and keep it ice cold. Freeze part of the eggnog mixture and add to the punch bowl just before serving.

EGGS: The egg nutritionally is a nearly perfect food. They are in fact, one of nature's phenomena, containing protein, minerals, fats, traces of carbohydrates and vitamins.

Although a complete food in their own right, eggs are used to thicken custards and puddings; to leaven spongecakes, omelets and souffles; to bind meat loaves and casseroles; to emulsify mayonnaise and salad dressing; to clarify consomme; to garnish canapes, salads and soups; and to add color and taste to sauces and cakes.

To achieve the very best results, freshness is a must. There are two methods for testing freshness: 1) drop egg gently into deep cold water; if fresh, egg will sink to bottom and lie on its side. Old eggs lose part of their content by evaporation and will not lie flat. 2) hold egg before a flashlight in a dimly lit room. If the center is clear, the egg is fresh. This is called candling.

Use only clean, sound eggs. Cracked or soiled eggs may contain bacteria that can produce food poisoning.

Store eggs away from strongly scented foods, egg shells are porous and absorb odors.

For less breakage, store eggs with broad ends up.

Add salt to egg dishes after they are cooked, salt has a tendency to toughen eggs.

The secret for success in preparing eggs and dishes in which eggs predominate is to cook slowly at moderate, even temperatures.

Never use extra-large eggs for baking cakes. They cause cake to fall when cooled. Use either large or medium.

Boiled Eggs: The way *not* to cook an egg is to grab it out of the refrigerator and drop it into fast boiling water. Actually, eggs should never be boiled! High temperatures and fast boiling make eggwhites shrink, lose moisture and taste mushy.

To soft cook an egg properly, place it in a saucepan and cover it with cold water. Salt added to water helps keep egg from cracking. Place the saucepan over high heat and bring the water to a boil. Then turn off heat, cover pan, and let the egg stand from 2 to 4 minutes, according to taste.

To hard cook eggs, let stand in the water for fifteen minutes, remove and then immediately cool under cold running water. Fast cooling helps to avoid a greenish tinge around the edge of the yolk.

To slice hard cooked eggs without breaking the yolk, dip knife into water before slicing.

Try pickling whole hard cooked eggs by placing them in a jar and covering with the juice of pickled beets. Pink pickled eggs make a luscious appetizer and adds sparkle to a table.

When boiling eggs, use an enameled saucepan and a wooden spoon. Aluminum spoons and pots turn green.

Poached Eggs: Cold eggs poach better than eggs at room temperature. The white does not spread as much when the egg is broken but remains around the yolk.

61

A few drops of vinegar added to the cooking water will keep poached eggs from running all over the pan.

To make your own easy egg poacher, remove the top and bottom from an empty tuna fish can and wash the can-ring thoroughly. Place the can ring in the water and gently slide egg in the center.

Always use a wooden spoon for stirring eggs, a metal spoon turns eggs grayish.

To prevent eggs from sticking to pan, heat pan first before adding butter or oil.

Eggs beat up fluffier at room temperature, remove from refrigerator thirty minutes before using.

Omelets: For fluffier omelets, beat egg yolks and whites separately.

For a more tender omelet, use hot water instead of milk in the recipe.

Never make an omelet with more than four eggs at a time. Omelets require even heat and room to expand.

The pan used for omelets should have a thick base and be approximately two inches deep.

When making a cheese omelet, add the cheese immediately before folding the omelet.

Separate eggs while cold, the yolks are less likely to break.

Fried Eggs: Give a better appearance to a fried egg by breaking it first in a saucer and then gently slide it into the hot pan.

Scrambled Eggs: Give a better appearance to scrambled eggs by lifting them gently with a spatula from the bottom of the pan and turn slowly instead of stirring.

Soufflé: A delicate, fluffy baked dish made light by the addition of stiffly beaten egg whites before baking.

For successful soufflés, sauce must be thick and smooth. Egg whites should be folded into sauce in two equal portions; the first half blended thoroughly, the last half only partially.

Soufflé dish should be buttered and dusted with confectioner's sugar.

Never open the oven door until five minutes before the end of the cooking time. A cold draft will collapse it.

Always serve a soufflé immediately; it cannot be prepared in advance.

Eggwhites: eight eggwhites equal one cup.

One eggwhite fits perfectly in an individual ice

cube container. Once frozen, remove from container and store in freezer bag. Thaw and use exactly as you would a fresh eggwhite. Eggwhites can be kept frozen for up to one year.

When beating eggwhites for meringue, beat in sugar one tablespoon at a time until very stiff and glossy.

Always whip egg whites at high speed for greater volume.

For firmer egg whites, add a dash of cream of tartar before whipping.

A copper bowl works wonders for whisking egg whites.

Eggwhites make a wonderful beauty mask. Just spread thinly over the face, allow it to dry and wash off with warm water.

Eggwhite poured over a burn holds down the inflammation and relieves the pain. The colder the eggwhite, the better.

Leftover yolks should be covered with cold water and refrigerated in a tightly covered container to prevent yolks from sticking together.

For egg whites which have specks of yolk in them, use the cut edge of the shell to scoop out the speck. It is impossible to remove yolk from white with anything but its own shell.

Crushed eggshells mixed with water makes a super fertilizer for your houseplants. Simply fill glass jar halfway with crumbled eggshells and add water to top. Cover tightly and let stand for three weeks in a dark place. Water your house plants with this mixture and watch them take on a new life!

EGGPLANT: Select eggplants that are heavy, firm, smooth, glossy and dark in color.

A medium sized eggplant (1 1/2 pounds) serves four.

Unpeeled eggplant holds its shape better in cooking. Peel only if the skin is tough.

To prevent darkening of cut eggplant, dip the pieces as soon as possible into the coating, liquid or fat called for in the recipe.

ELECTRIC FRYPANS AND SKILLETS: Heat is thermostatically controlled. Therefore, food does not have to be watched constantly.

Select unit with high-domed lids which will permit pot roasting and cake baking as well.

Select unit with heating elements in lid to allow broiling in the fry pan.

Select unit with crockery inserts to make skillet a slow-cooker.

EMULSION: A liquid preparation resembling milk in which minute particles remain in suspension, as fatty globules in milk.

EN BROCHETTE: Meats cooked, and often served, on a skewer.

ENDIVE: Select crisp, fresh, tender plants. Avoid tough, dark green outer leaves.

Endive can be used interchangeably with escarole in salads and in cooking.

Belgian endive has white leaves with light green tips and a slightly bitter flavor.

Curly endive grows in a loose leaf head. It is a plant with narrow, finely divided, curly leaves and a slightly bitter taste.

See also **SALAD.**

ESCALOPE: *See* **SCALOPPINE.**

ESCARGOT: An edible variety of snail.

ESCAROLE: A salad green with broad waved leaves, slightly bitter to the taste.

Select crisp, tender leaves with no brown edges. Leaves should be easily snapped and have a yellow-green color.

Can be used interchangeably with endive in salads and in cooking.

See also **SALAD.**

ESPRESSO: A very strong, rich, dark brew of coffee ground extra fine from coffee beans that have been roasted extra dark.

Usually served in demitasse cups.

Usually served with twists of lemon peel but tasty variations may be served with heavy cream, vanilla ice cream or a lacing of liqueurs.

F

FENNEL: An herb very similar to celery and may be used as a substitute in recipes calling for celery as seasoning.

Delicious raw as a relish, or cooked in soups and stews.

See also **HERBS & SPICE.**

FIGS: Store fresh figs in the refrigerator as soon as possible. They are very perishable.

Pare off the outer skin with a sharp knife, skin is not edible.

Fully ripe figs are naturally sweet, need no additional sweetener.

Keep dried figs in a tightly covered container in a cool place to prevent loss of moisture.

For a change of pace, soak dried figs in wine instead of water for zesty flavor.

FILBERT: *See* **HAZELNUT** and **NUTS.**

FILLET: To bone and slice fish or meat.

A boneless, lean piece of fish or meat.

FINNAN HADDIE: Finnan haddie is actually smoked haddock.

One pound finnan haddie yields two cups cooked, flaked fish.

To improve the flavor of finnan haddie when cooking, add one-quarter cup sweet cream.

FISH: I was discussing ways to prepare fish with a French chef, for whom I have great admiration. Over the years we have exchanged many ideas, mostly his, about everything pertaining to food. However, concerning fish, his first instructions were: Take a live fish and kill it by striking it sharply on the head! I never heard another word he said. I prefer to think of fish jumping into nets by themselves and expiring with a smile on their face from whatever turned them on! For the faint of heart, such as myself, I lovingly give the following fish cues.

When shopping for fresh fish, choose whole fish with clear bulging eyes, free of any browning around the edges, and with a texture elastic and firm enough to leave no dimple mark if pressed with a finger. Gray or greenish coloring is a sign of aging in fish.

Fresh fish should be kept covered in refrigerator, in a bowl with crushed ice to preserve freshness.

If you think fish smells funny, when in doubt—throw it out!

Frozen fish should be fully thawed to room temperature and dried on absorbent paper before using.

Never defrost fish in water, all the water soluble vitamins will be lost.

Thaw fish in milk, it provides a fresh caught flavor.

It takes six hours to defrost fish in the refrigerator and about two hours at room temperature.

Never refreeze fish that has been thawed. Cook at once and serve or store in refrigerator.

Fish cooks best when arranged in a single layer in any cooking vessel.

Fat fishes are more desirable for baking and broiling (whitefish, salmon, red snapper).

Lean fish may be broiled or baked if basted frequently with butter or margarine.

The fine rule of thumb for cooking fish, whether baked or poached, is to measure the thickness of the filet with a small ruler at its thickest point. Allow ten minutes of cooking time for each inch of thickness but do not overcook. Fish is ready to serve when the flesh is easily flaked with a fork. Overcooking makes fish tough and dry.

Fish should be seasoned gently, its delicate flavor can be easily overwhelmed when heavily spiced.

To preserve shape and texture when poaching fish, the liquid must be just below the boiling point so that it barely simmers. It should not cover the fish

For a different and zesty taste when boiling or poaching fish, try beer for the liquid.

For the easiest and best garnish for any cooked fish, try combining 1/4 cup drained and chopped capers with 1/4 cup pitted and chopped green olives.

When frying fish, a few slices of an apple placed in the pan while cooking will hold down the fishy cooking odor.

Average fish servings are:

	Servings per pound[1]
Whole...................................	1 or 2
Dressed or pan-dressed...................	2 or 3
Portions or steaks.......................	3
Fillets..................................	3 or 4

[1]Three ounces of cooked lean fish per serving.

Timetable for cooking fish:

Cooking method and market form	Approximate ready-to-cook weight or thickness	Cooking temperature	Approximate cooking time in minutes
BAKING			
Dressed . . . . 3 pounds . . . . 350° F.			45 to 60
Pan-dressed. . . . . 3 pounds . . . . 350° F.			25 to 30
Fillets or steaks. . . . . . 2 pounds . . . . 350° F.			20 to 25
Portions. . . . . 2 pounds . . . . 400° F.			15 to 20
Sticks. . . . . 2 1/4 pounds . . . . . . 400° F.			15 to 20
BROILING			
Pan-dressed. . . . . 3 pounds			10 to 16[1]
Fillets or steaks. . . . . . 1/2 to 1 inch.			10 to 15
Portions. . . . . 3/8 to 1/2 inch.			10 to 15
Sticks. . . . . 3/8 to 1/2 inch.			10 to 15
CHARCOAL BROILING			
Pan-dressed. . . . . 3 pounds . . . . Moderate . . .			10 to 16[1]
Fillets or steaks. . . . . . 1/2 to 1 inch. . . . . . . Moderate . . .			10 to 16[1]
Portions. . . . . 3/8 to 1/2 inch. . . . . Moderate . . .			8 to 10[1]
Sticks. . . . . 3/8 to 1/2 inch. . . . . Moderate . . .			8 to 10[1]
DEEP-FAT FRYING			
Pan-dressed. . . . . 3 pounds . . . . 350° F.			3 to 5
Fillets or steaks. . . . . . 1/2 to 1 inch. . . . . . . 350° F.			3 to 5
Portions. . . . . 3/8 to 1/2 inch. . . . . 350° F.			3 to 5
Sticks. . . . . 3/8 to 1/2 inch. . . . . 350° F.			3 to 5
OVEN-FRYING			
Pan-dressed. . . . . 3 pounds . . . . 500° F.			15 to 20
Fillets or steaks. . . . . . 1/2 to 1 inch. . . . . . . 500° F.			10 to 15

Pan-dressed	3 pounds	Moderate	8 to 10[1]
Fillets or steaks	1/2 to 1 inch	Moderate	8 to 10[1]
Portions	3/8 to 1/2 inch	Moderate	8 to 10[1]
Sticks	3/8 to 1/2 inch	Moderate	8 to 10[1]

POACHING

Fillets or steaks	2 pounds	Simmer	5 to 10

STEAMING

Fillets or steaks	2 pounds	Boil	5 to 10

---

[1]Turn once.

To remove fish odor from hands or utensils, rub with salt and wash with cold water.

See individual types of fish.

FLAMBÉ: Describing foods which are served flaming.

For successful flaming, liquors should be heated before igniting.

The most popular liquors for flaming are brandy, rum and kirsh.

For safety, ignite at table—never attempt to carry a flaming dish.

FLAN: An open faced tart with any savory or sweet filling.

A custard or caramel cream thickened with eggs or other thickening agents.

FLANK: A section of beef taken from the side of the animal between the ribs and hip.

FLOATING ISLAND: A soft custard dessert topped with puffs of meringue.

FLORENTINE: A la Florentine is a style of cooking which uses spinach as the base and is then baked or broiled.

FLOUNDER: Generally a lean fish.

To clean, wash quickly in salted water. Do not soak or flounder may lose flavor and nutrients.

When baking or broiling, baste frequently to prevent dryness.

See also **FISH.**

FLOUR: To maintain freshness, store flour in a cool dry place in a tightly closed container.

All Purpose Flour is made of a mixture of hard and soft wheat, rich in gluten. It is good for thickening sauces and gravies since it cooks smoothly with no danger of lumping.

Pastry Flour is finely milled flour, low in gluten and is more delicate than All Purpose. Excellent for pastry and fine cakes.

Cake Flour is made of soft wheats with less gluten than pastry flour, thus giving a very fine textured cake.

To substitute All Purpose flour for Pastry or Cake flour, reduce the amount by two tablespoons per cup.

FLUKE: A salt water flatfish also known as summer flounder. Fluke can weigh between one and fifteen pounds and can be used interchangeably with any recipe calling for flounder.

See also **FLOUNDER** and **FISH.**

FLUMMERY: Berries simmered in water and thickened with cornstarch.

FOLD: To combine ingredients by blending with a spoon or whisk in a gentle up-and-over motion.

FONDUE: A hot dish, usually melted cheese, into which pieces of bread or other foods are dipped before eating.

The fondue pot is kept warm at the table while all guests dip their choice of delicacies into the bubbling fondue.

A chocolate fondue makes a festive party dessert with an assortment of sweets such as fresh fruit, marshmallows, etc. used for dipping.

FOOD PROCESSORS: Processors can grate, slice, chop, blend, puree, grind, knead, shred, and mix pastry and bread doughs easily and quickly.

FRENCH FRIED: For perfect french frying, make sure food is dry and of uniform size before cooking

Heat fat slowly. To test for correct temperature, drop in cube of day-old bread. If bread browns in twenty seconds (count to twenty), the fat is ready.

When french frying potatoes, soak them in cold water for better results but be sure to drain well before frying.

FRENCH TOAST: For tastier toast, add one teaspoon of vanilla extract to egg/milk mixture before dipping.

For unusual toast, cut slices of toast into finger shapes about one-inch wide.

FRICASSE: To cook by braising; usually applied to fowl, rabbit or cut-up veal.

FRITTER: A tiny portion of batter either mixed with chopped cooked fish, meat, fruit or vegetables or used as a coating for these foods.

For perfect fritters, make sure food is dry before coating and completely coated before frying.

For a fluffier fritter coating beat egg whites separately and add to batter last.

Keep batter thin for delicate and crisp fritters—add liquid to thin out batter.

FROGS' LEGS: Resembles chicken in texture and flavor although somewhat milder.

Only the hind legs are used. Allow two large or six to eight small legs per serving.

For easier dressing, chill before skinning. When skinning, begin at top and strip off the skin as you would a glove.

To improve flavor, soak legs in cold milk for two hours, drain and dry before cooking.

Requires very short cooking time. To prevent toughness, do not overcook.

FROSTING: If boiled icing hardens too soon, beat in a teaspoon of boiling water to soften.

Add nuts or raisins to boiled icing at the very last minute. The oil or acid in nuts or raisins is apt to thin the icing if added too soon.

For a more attractive frosted cake, reverse cakes that have uneven tops and ice the bottoms.

For easier cutting of iced layer cakes, dip the blade of the knife in warm water occasionally. Slice with up and down motions for best results.

See also **CAKES**.

FRUIT: Good fresh fruit is one of the best of desserts, whether served plain or adorned with liqueur. It can appear at any point during a meal as an appetizer, in a salad, or as a light dessert to top off a heavy meal. Fruits are comparatively low in calories and rewarding in high food values.

To help unripened fruit ripen faster, place in a loosely closed brown bag at room temperature.

Must be washed very carefully due to the strong sprays used on fruit trees.

Always peel and cut fruit with a stainless steel knife to prevent discoloration.

To prevent fruits from darkening after being peeled, dip them in any citrus juice.

Marinate fresh fruit in 2 cups of sweet port wine for one hour for a gourmet taste and touch.

Prick fruit before tossing with liqueur to allow flavor to penetrate.

A small amount of cinnamon, lemon, nutmeg or vanilla adds an extra spark to poaching or marinating fruit.

See also individual fruits.

FRY: To cook in fat.

FRYER: *See* **BROILER.**

FUDGE: To prevent fudge from crystallizing, stir with a wooden spoon instead of a metal one.

To prevent fudge from running over, butter the rim of the pot.

For smooth and creamy fudge, select a recipe which utilizes corn syrup (the secret weapon in good fudge).

For easy marshmallow fudge, add miniature marshmallows to fudge just before pouring into pan.

GAME: Any wild bird judged to be suitable for table use such as grouse, partridge, pheasant, wild duck, wild goose, quail, woodcock, snipe and plover.

As a rule of thumb, allow one pound per serving.

Apt to be lean with a tendency to dry out during cooking. Therefore, lard game to prevent dryness.

GARLIC: For freshness, select firm, plump buds with clean, dry, unbroken skins.

Store away from other foods in a cool dry place to prevent its strong odors from affecting other foods.

Halve a clove of garlic and rub the inside of salad bowl for added zest to salads.

1/8 teaspoon garlic powder or 1/2 teaspoon garlic salt equals one medium clove garlic.

To make garlic salt, split a clove of garlic and crush it with one teaspoon of salt.

GARNISH: An ornament, preferably edible, added to a finished dish for the purpose of enhancing its appearance.

GELATIN: One tablespoon unflavored gelatin molds two cups of liquid.

One three-ounce package flavored gelatin molds two cups of liquid.

To chill gelatin quickly, place in freezer for ten minutes, stirring occasionally, until desired consistency.

Fruits that float in gelatin are apple cubes, peach and pear slices, strawberries, melon balls, blueberries, banana slices and mandarin oranges.

Fruits that sink in gelatin are fresh grapes, oranges, plums, cooked prunes and all fruits canned in heavy syrup.

Pineapple must be boiled for two minutes to destroy the protein digesting enzyme in pineapple which prevents jelling before adding to gelatin.

For best results, whip gelatin mixtures that are nearly set at medium speed.

For better molded gelatins, dip molds in cold water before filling but be sure to shake out all loose drops of water.

Gelatin salad molds should first be brushed with olive oil for easier removal.

To unmold gelatin, quickly lower mold into a bowl of

very hot water. Lift mold and with point of small knife, loosen sides. Place large platter over top of mold and hold platter and mold tightly together. Turn upside down and set platter gently on a flat surface. Lift off mold—SHAZAM!! If it doesn't work, do not despair but start all over again.

GENOISE: A multi-layered cake filled with butter creme and usually decorated with slivered almonds. Luscious!

GHERKIN: Very small cucumber used to make either sweet or sour pickles.

GIBLETS: The gizzard, liver and heart of any kind of poultry.

GINGER: A peppery tasting spice widely used for flavoring ginger ale, soups, meat, poultry dishes and especially for baking gingerbread. Very popular in Chinese style cooking.

See also **HERBS & SPICES.**

GINGERBREAD: A flat, square, spicy bread/cake, spiced with ground ginger and other spices.

GLACE: A coating of sugar or sugar syrup used on fruits, cakes and breads. Glazing may also be done with sauce, butter or gelatin.

GLAZE: To cover food with a mixture which hardens and becomes glossy. Glaze gives an attractive finish to either hot or cold dishes.

GNOCCHI: An Italian dumpling.

GOOSE: Select fresh geese with a good layer of fat and soft, clean, unbruised skin. A pliable upper bill is an indication of a young bird.

Allow 1 1/2 pounds per person per serving. Goose has much bone and fat in proportion to the meat.

Prick the breast skin of the goose in several places to allow fat to drain away.

For crisp goose skin, rub goose inside and out with lemon halves before roasting.

A ten pound goose requires eight cups of stuffing.

As a rule of thumb, sharp spices and dry stuffings are tastiest with geese.

GOULASH: A thick stew that always contains meat, onions and sweet or hot paprika.

GRAPEFRUIT: For juiciest grapefruits, select those that are smooth, thin-skinned and heavy for their size.

Store in the refrigerator to avoid drying and wrinkling.

For easier squeezing, grapefruits should be at room temperature.

GRAPES: Select grapes that are plump, fresh in appearance and firmly attached to the stems.

Store grapes in perforated plastic bags in refrigerator to keep fresh. They require air to maintain freshness.

See also **FRUIT.**

GRATE: To grind food into shreds or particles of appropriate coarseness.

GRAVY: For clear gravy, thicken with one tablespoon cornstarch instead of flour.

For a rich brown gravy, cook the flour thoroughly with the fat before adding any liquid.

Use a blending fork to keep gravy smooth.

In the event lumps form in gravy, pour through a strainer and discard lumps.

For pale looking, unappetizing gravy, add brewed black coffee until desired color is achieved.

For a change of pace, thicken gravy with one cup of flavored bread crumbs to two cups gravy.

For gravy that is too salty, add a few teaspoons of instant mashed potatoes. Thin, if necessary, with a little hot water.

Canned soups make an excellent base for many gravies.

GREASE: Spreading a pan thinly with fat to keep foods from sticking during cooking or baking.

GREENS: Any wild or cultivated green herbage which is eaten raw or cooked.

GRENADINE: A non-alcholic French syrup made from the juice of pomegranates.

GRIDDLE CAKES: A thin, round pancake made from batter and cooked on a griddle.

For tastier griddle cakes, beat the batter only until it is just smooth. Overbeating causes toughness.

Generally served with butter and an assortment of syrups.

To test griddle for proper cooking temperature, drop a little water on it. If water sizzles and bounces, griddle is ready.

To keep warm for a short time, place in a covered towel in a 200 degree oven.

GRIND: To put food through a food chopper.

GRITS (or GROATS): Hulled and coarsely ground cereal grains.

Grits ground from corn are known as Hominy Grits.

Groats are most often ground from oats, barley, wheat and corn.

Buckwheat groats are known as Kasha, a staple food of Russia.

GRUEL: Cereal boiled with water to the consistency of a thin porridge.

GRUNION: A small, salt water fish, similar to the smelt.

GUMBO: A thick soup made with okra pods and other vegetables.

GUMDROP: A soft candy made from sugar and water with flavoring and color added.

HALF & HALF: A dairy product consisting of a mixture of milk and cream.

HALIBUT: Halibut may be cooked by dry moist heat, broiled, poached, baked, fried or used for souffle or steamed pudding.

Chicken halibut, weighing up to ten pounds, is excellent in flavor and texture and is considered to be the finest eating variety.

Any deviled sauce adds zest to halibut due to its bland flavor.

See also **FISH.**

HAM: The rear leg of a hog, from the hipbone through the meaty part of the shank bone.

Purchase one-third pound per serving of boneless ham.

Purchase one pound per serving for bone-in fresh ham.

Fresh ham should be cooked at low temperatures to destroy any trichinae organisms present. Completely cooked it should be grayish-white in color without any tinge of pink.

Precooked hams take ten minutes per pound to heat thoroughly in a 350 degree oven.

See also **PORK.**

HAMBURGER: *See* **BEEF.**

HARD SAUCE: A sauce made by creaming butter with sugar and flavoring it with brandy, rum, whisky, wine or spices.

For easier creaming, add one tablespoon of cream to butter/sugar mixture before flavoring it.

To stiffen sauce, chill in refrigerator for two hours.

HARDTACK: A large, hard biscuit made of unsalted dough and dried after baking.

HASENPFEFFER: A highly seasoned marinated stew of rabbit.

HASH: A mixture of foods chopped into small pieces and mixed together.

HAZELNUT: Also known as filberts.

One pound shelled nuts yields 3 1/2 cups nutmeats.

Hazelnuts are brittle. For easy shelling, use a nut-cracker.

To make a hazelnut paste, use a meat grinder for quick results.

See also **NUTS.**

HEAD CHEESE: A well seasoned cold cut made from the edible parts of a calf's or pig's head.

HERBS & SPICES: Can add a zesty new flavor to a variety of ordinary dishes. It is important not to add too much. No recipe can do more than suggest the right amount since seasonings depend on individual taste. Use discretion, season to enhance the flavor of a dish, not to overpower it.

Herbs are plants with succulent, distinctly flavored leaves which can be used fresh or dried. Some more commonly used herbs are:

Basil—flavor resembling cloves.
Bay Leaves—always included in bouquet garni.
Chervil—delicate flavor resembles both parsley and fennel.
Chives—related to onions and similar in flavor.
Dill—used mostly in pickling.
Fennel—related to the parsley plant with a flavor similar to aniseed.
Marjoram—a sweet herb.
Mint—usually used fresh.
Oregano—essential in Latin cookery.
Parsley—a lacy green herb with a slightly sharp flavor.
Rosemary—mint flavored.
Sage—commonly used in poultry stuffing.
Sorrel—essentially a French herb.
Tarragon—can be used fresh in salads.
Thyme—pungently flavored.

Spices are aromatic parts of plants which are dried and used either whole or in pulverized form. Some more commonly used spices are:

Allspice—from the pimento tree with a flavor similar to a mixture of cinnamon, cloves and nutmeg.

Caraway Seeds—used whole.

Cardamon Seeds—resemble anise in flavor.

Celery Seeds—used in pickling and soups.

Cinnamon—used either in the ground form or in whole, large pieces.

Cloves—available either whole or ground.

Coriander Seeds—comes in powdered form and is a constituent of curry powder.

Cumin Seed—comes in ground form and is a constituent of curry paste.

Ginger—available in pieces of stem, crystallized, or in ground form.

Mace—the covering of the nutmeg with a similar delicate flavor.

Mustard Seeds—comes in black and white with the ground form used mainly in making a condiment or relish.

Nutmeg—available either ground or as whole seeds.

Pepper—both black and white are obtained from the same plant; the black from the dried immature fruit and the white from the dried mature fruit with the hull removed.

Saffron—from a plant related to the crocus.

Sesame Seeds—have a nutty flavor.

Turmeric—a yellow powder used extensively in curry powder and prepared mustards.

Vanilla—a delicate flavoring for sweet dishes.

Should be stored in tightly closed containers. Long exposure to heat, moisture or air should be avoided.

Purchase the smallest package available. Herbs and spices begin to lose their strength after opening.

Use fresh herbs whenever possible. Dried herbs are almost as good but are three-times stronger than fresh, so measure accordingly.

Always crumble herbs before using to release flavor.

To bring out flavor of dried herbs, soak them in lemon juice for a few minutes before adding to any recipe.

Long cooking destroys the flavor of ground herbs and spices so add these during the last hour of cooking in dishes such as soups or stews. Whole spices may be added at the beginning.

Add herbs to sauces at the last minute so that their essential oils are not evaporated.

A stronger infusion results when fresh herbs are soaked in two tablespoons of milk for one hour before adding to ground meat. Add the milk as well for juicier results. May be done with dried herbs as well as alternate method to lemon juice soaking indicated previously.

In uncooked foods, such as salad dressing or desserts,

spices are added well in advance of serving to permit the flavors to "marry" by standing a few hours to bring out flavor.

HERMIT: A dark, spicy cookie filled with fruit and nuts.

HERRING: To eliminate salt in brine-packed herring, soak in fresh water for twenty-four hours before using. Change water several times.

Prepare fresh herring as you would any other fish. *See* **FISH.**

Garnish rollmops (rolled-up pickled herring) with fancy frilled toothpicks for a festive treat.

See also **SMOKED FISH.**

HOECAKE: A cornmeal cake baked in a frying pan or on a griddle.

HOLLANDAISE: Sauce made from eggs and butter, served hot or cold, over vegetables or fish.

HOMINY GRITS: *See* **GRITS.**

HOMOGENIZE: To reduce an emulsion to particles of the same size and to distribute them evenly. The term is applied to milk, salad dressings and mayonnaise.

HONEY: For honey that has crystallized, stand jar in a pan of hot water until it liquefies.

For easier measuring and pouring, heat honey first.

To substitute honey for sugar, deduct one-quarter cup of liquid used in recipe for each cup of honey utilized. Honey contains water which necessitates liquid adjustment in recipe.

HONEYDEW MELON: Select melons with creamy yellow rinds, soft to the touch and with a sweet odor.

Ripen melons at room temperature away from the sun.

Always serve ice-cold for peak flavor.

HORS d'OEUVRES: Unlike canapes, hors d'oeuvres do *not* use bread as a base.

May be served hot or cold but always in small portions.

Hors d'oeuvres should be served *at* the table before the main part of the meal but should never repeat the ingredients of the main dish. For example, if fish is being served as main course, avoid seafood hors d'oeuvres.

HORSERADISH: Grate fresh horseradish as soon as possible after purchase for peak taste. Horseradish loses its zest with age.

To reconstitute dried horseradish, add two tablespoons of water to each tablespoon of dried horse-radish.

One grated sour apple adds a sweet/sour taste to fresh grated horseradish.

HOT CAKES: *See* **GRIDDLE CAKES.**

HUCKLEBERRY: Select plump, dry berries with deep black color for freshness.

Wash gently just before using as water washes away flavor. Do not soak.

Interchangeable in any recipe calling for blueberries.

ICE CREAM: A frozen food made from milk products, sweetening, flavoring and other ingredients.

For homemade ice cream, crank freezing gives velvety texture. Freezer can should be scalded and rinsed with cold water each time it is used.

A two-quart freezer is average size (either electric or hand-cranked).

To allow for expansion, pour chilled ice cream mixture in the can no more than two-thirds full.

To hasten freezing use a larger portion of salt when preparing, but ice cream will then be less velvety.

To stiffen ice cream that refuses to harden, stir in beaten egg whites when the ice cream is frozen to a mushy texture and then continue freezing.

ICE CUBES: To avoid ice cubes sticking together, try storing them in freezer in a brown paper bag.

For decorative ice cubes, place a maraschino cherry or a sprig of mint in each section of the ice tray and then freeze.

Flavor ice cubes by adding juice to the water before freezing. Delicious in lemonade, iced tea, etc.

ICED COFFEE: For a fast and easy dessert, add a scoop of vanilla ice cream on top of iced coffee.

Freeze brewed coffee into cubes for an undiluted iced coffee treat.

ICED TEA: Try freezing lemonade into cubes for an undiluted iced tea treat.

Add one-quart of gingerale to one-quart of iced tea for an unusual flavored iced tea.

For zestier flavor, try adding one teaspoon of rum to each serving of iced tea.

ICES: Made from sweetened fruit juices, usually diluted with water.

To make successful ices, beat partially frozen ices until evenly blended, then spoon back into the tray and freeze until firm.

Ices freeze well in plain refrigerator trays in freezer.

ICING: *See* **FROSTING** and **CAKES.**

INDIAN PUDDING: A pudding made with cereal.

For the finest flavor, use the best and darkest molasses you can find.

Do not overcook. Indian pudding should be soft and separate somewhat.

For added zest, try serving with vanilla ice cream.

IRISH COFFEE: A hot strong coffee laced with Irish whisky, some sugar, and topped with whipped cream.

JAM: Made from crushed fruits and cooked with sugar until the mixture is blended and thick.

For best results, cook in small quantities, no more than four cups at a time.

For proper measurements in making jam, use one cup of sugar to one cup of acid fruit, or three-quarters cup sugar to one cup of non-acid fruit.

To prevent jam from sticking to the pot, grease pot with olive oil.

JAMBALAYA: A New Orleans Creole dish made from combinations of ham, fowl, sausage, shrimp, oysters, tomatoes, rice, onions, garlic and other seasonings.

A spicy main dish such as Jambalaya is best served with a simple green salad and a very plain dessert to complete the meal.

JELLY: Made by cooking extracted fruit juices with sugar. A clear, delicately tender but not syrupy substance which holds its shape when unmolded.

JULEP: An alcoholic drink most often made with bourbon, sugar, crushed ice and mint.

For a frosty look on the outside, chill goblets or tumblers in the freezer before adding crushed ice.

JULIENNE: Food cut into thin match-like strips.

K

KABOB: Small pieces of meat, fish or poultry, with or without vegetables or fruits, which are threaded on skewers and then broiled or roasted.

KALE: When buying this vegetable, select crisp-looking fresh leaves.

To properly cook, remove the tough stems and midribs; cut large leaves into pieces.

Kale may be cooked in any of the ways spinach is prepared but allow more time for kale leaves to become tender.

Crisp, crumbled bacon adds zest to cooked kale.

See also **VEGETABLES.**

KASHA: *See* **GRITS.**

KIDNEY BEANS: One cup dried kidney beans serves four since dried beans double in bulk when cooked.

To prevent beans from darkening an aluminum pot, add one-quarter teaspoon vinegar or lemon juice.

If desired, rub the inside of the pot with a cut onion before cooking to lightly flavor the beans with onion.

See also **DRIED BEANS.**

KIDNEYS: For tastier kidneys, split and remove the whole white tubes and the fat before cooking.

Allow one pork kidney; one veal kidney, or two lamb kidneys per serving. One beef kidney will serve three.

Pork kidneys should be sliced and cooked at least 1 1/2 hours to assure thorough cooking.

Veal, lamb or beef kidneys should not be overcooked. Overcooking causes toughness.

KNEAD: A motion of mixing with the palms and heels of the hands to make dough smooth.

KNOCKWURST: A smoked and cooked sausage with ingredients similar to the frankfurter but contains more garlic. Larger around and shorter in length than the frankfurter.

May be eaten as is or cooked to taste.

KOHLRABI: This vegetable should be selected small in size with fresh tops. Large heads are woody.

Has a flavor not unlike that of a crisp radish when young and tender. Delicious sliced in mixed salads.

Allow two small heads per person.

May be eaten fresh, boiled, stuffed or added to soups and stews.

KIELBASI: A highly seasoned sausage made of pork and beef and flavored with spices.

Sold in straight links about four to five inches long and about 1 1/2 inches wide.

For peak taste, should be simmered for thirty minutes or until well done.

KISSES: A meringe type cookie.

For better results, use eggs that are one week old.

To prevent sticking, wipe the back of the paper on which cookies are baked with a damp cloth before baking.

KUMQUATS: Kumquats are tastier cooked in preserves or pickled rather than eaten raw.

Ripe kumquats make a pretty garnish on a fruit cup or salad.

L

LAMB: A young sheep of either sex that is under one year of age and therefore a tender meat.

Flesh should be pinkish, firm and finely grained. Fat should be white, solid and flaky.

Lamb rule of thumb serving portions are:

	Servings per pound[1]
Much bone or gristle...............................	1 or 2
Medium amounts of bone..........................	2 or 3
Little or no bone..................................	3 or 4

[1]Three ounces of cooked lean meat per serving.

Loin lamb chops are usually cut three to the pound. They should be broiled two inches below heat for chops cut 1-1 1/2 inches and three inches below heat for thicker cuts.

Shoulder lamb chops should be cut about one inch thick. Broil as lamb chops.

Kidney lamb chops are loin chops with kidney attached.

Lamb steaks—ask your butcher for one-inch slices cut from the leg.

Crown roast—a double piece of the loin has fourteen chops, perfect for a crown of lamb. On the average, allow two ribs per person.

When preparing, keep the tips from blackening by wrapping with a bit of aluminum foil.

A crown roast should be pinkish, not too well done. Roast in a 325 degree oven for about two hours for best results.

Leg of lamb—a four pound leg will produce two pounds of edible meat.

When carving, cut one-half inch slices for average servings.

Lamb variety meats available are brains, heart, kidneys, liver, tongue and sweetbreads.

Mint jelly is the expected accompaniment to lamb.

Timetables for cooking lamb:

BRAISING

Kind and cut of meat	Approximate ready-to-cook weight or thickness	Approximate total cooking time
		Hours
Chops..................	1/2 to 3/4 inch....	1/2 to 3/4
Shanks.................	1 pound each......	1 1/2 to 2
Shoulder, rolled..........	3 to 5 pounds......	2 to 2 1/2

BROILING

Kind and cut of meat	Approximate thickness	Degree of doneness	Approximate total cooking time[1]
	Inches		*Minutes*
Lamb chops..........	1	Medium....	12
(Loin, rib, shoulder)	1	Well done..	14
	1 1/2	Medium....	18
	1 1/2	Well done..	22

[1]Meat at refrigerator temperature at start of broiling.

Kind and cut of meat	Ready-to-cook weight	Approximate roasting time at 325° F.	Internal temperature of meat when done
	Pounds	*Hours*	*°F.*
Leg (whole)............	6 to 7	3 1/4 to 4	180
Shoulder..............	3 to 6	2 1/4 to 3 1/4	180
Rolled shoulder........	3 to 5	2 1/2 to 3	180

LARD: Pork fat which has been rendered and clarified.

To substitute lard for butter in cooking, use twenty percent less lard than butter.

Pastry made with lard is especially flaky.

LARDING: A process for making dry meat tastier with the insertion of long strips of pork or ham.

If you do not own a larding needle, meat can be larded with an icepick or thick knitting needle. Insert pick or needle into meat and push through strips of pork or ham.

LASAGNA: A broad noodle, approximately two inches wide with a ruffled or plain edge.

When boiling noodles, use three quarts of water and

two tablespoons of salt for each half-pound of dry noodles.

To prevent noodles from sticking to the pot, add one to two teaspoons of oil to the boiling water.

To prevent noodles from breaking while cooking, try cooking in electric skillet. Cover noodles with boiling water and cook required time.

Baked lasagna is a tasty Italian dish made with the lasagna noodles, cheese, tomato sauce, and variations which would include hard cooked eggs, meat, etc.
See also **PASTA.**

LAYER CAKE: A cake baked in layers, held together by a filling and covered with frosting.

LEAVEN: To add various substances which lighten dough or batter while it is baking (baking soda, baking powder, yeast, etc.).

LEBKUCHEN: One of the world's oldest spicecakes; of German origin.

LEEK: These vegetables should be selected with white lower part and green upper part.

One large bunch serves four.

For tastier leeks, trim the roots and part of the tops, leaving two-inches of green to remain before cooking.

LEMONS & LIMES: Select lemons and limes that are heavy for their size.

Smooth, thin skins usually indicate more juice.

Light or greenish-yellow lemons are more tart than those deep yellow in color.

To extract small amount of juice, puncture fruit with fork and gently squeeze out the desired amount.

To obtain maximum juice, firmly roll on a hard surface before squeezing.

Sprinkle over cut fruit to prevent it from darkening.

Lemon or lime baskets are easy to make and a most attractive part of your table setting. Just mark the outline on the lemon or lime with the point of a sharp knife. Then cut away the two upper quarters, leaving a strip about one-third inch wide to form the handle. Scoop out pulp carefully so that handle remains intact. Scallop edge of basket, if desired, fill with filling. Beautiful filled with mint jelly to serve with lamb.

LETTUCE: *Iceberg* lettuce has large, round and solid heads with medium green outer leaves and lighter green inner leaves.

Butterhead, Big Boston and *Bibb* lettuce have smaller heads with soft, tasty, light green leaves.

Leaf lettuce has a loose head and broad, fairly smooth, tender leaves which may vary in shades of green.

Romaine lettuce is tall and cylindrical with crisp, dark green leaves in a loosely folded head.

For parties, store large quantities of washed lettuce in a clean pillowcase in the refrigerator until needed.

To garnish lettuce leaves, sprinkle some paprika on waxed paper and dip edges of lettuce into it.

Any combination of lettuce may be deliciously combined with escarole, chicory, spinach or endive leaves.

See also **SALADS.**

LIQUEUR: Spirits that have been sweetened, flavored and occasionally colored according to their formula.

LIVER: One pounds serves four.

To prepare for cooking, wipe with a damp cloth and remove the thin outside skin and veins.

To panfry, purchase liver one-quarter inch thick.

To braise, purchase liver one-half inch thick.

To broil, purchase liver one-half inch thick.

LIVERWURST: A ready to eat sausage made of ground lean pork and pork liver mixed with spices and seasonings.

Darkens when sliced so therefore slice only as needed.

LOBSTER: The color of a live lobster is a dark mottled green. Only when cooked does it change to bright red.

Scientific evidence has shown a live lobster suffers less when put in cold water which is then brought to a boil rather than being plunged directly into boiling water. The flesh is also firmer and sweeter when done by this preferred method.

Two 1-pound lobsters yield one-half pound lobster meat.

For freshness, select cooked lobsters with tails that curl under the body when they are picked up.

LONDON BROIL: Also called flank steak.

Has long coarse fibers and must be cut across fibers when served.

LYONNAISE: Style of cooking for foods cooked with onions, especially potatoes.

MACARONI: For better taste, allow three quarts of water and one tablespoon of salt to cook eight ounces.

To prevent sticking, add one or two teaspoons of oil to the boiling water.

See also **PASTA.**

MACE: A spice with a similar flavor and odor of nutmeg but somewhat more pungent.

Used to flavor cake, custards, sauces, soups, poultry and fish.

Try adding a dash to oyster stew for that added zing.

See also **HERBS & SPICES.**

MACKEREL: Select mackerel with firm flesh, steely-blue skin and a fresh odor.

For better taste, wash mackerel under cold running water. Do not soak! Valuable flavor will be lost.

A four-pound baked or stuffed mackerel will serve 4.

See also **FISH.**

MADELEINE: A small delicate cake resembling a butter cookie, baked in a shell-shaped pan.

MADRILENE: A clear soup which is flavored with tomato juice and served cold.

MAIZE: A cereal grain known as Indian corn.

MANGOES: Fruit similar to cantaloupe but with a distinctive lemony flavor.

Select orange-yellow mangoes for ripeness.

For easier eating, cut ripe mangoes in half lengthwise and eat with a spoon.

Green mangoes are used in making chutney and pickles.

MARASCHINO: A sweet cherry which is bleached, pitted and steeped in syrup. Food coloring is added.

MARBLING: The depositing of fat around, between and within the muscles of meat which produces a mottled effect. Good marbling of meat contributes to the juiciness and flavor when it is cooked.

A contrast of color, usually light and dark, which is used to give a streaked appearance to cake batter.

MARINADE: A liquid mixture in which foods are soaked to give added flavor and tenderness.

MARINATE: To let foods stand in a marinade, usually a mixture of oil with vinegar or lemon juice, to add flavor or tenderize.

MARJORAM: A herb of the mint family, similar to thyme. Used to flavor pork, lamb, meat loaf, hash and stews.

See also **HERBS and SPICES.**

MARMALADES: Made from pulpy fruits, usually one or more citrus fruits, cut into large pieces and cooked so as to hold their shape in a thick, jellied, transparent syrup. Usually contain peel.

MARROW: The fatty filling in beef bones.

A squashlike edible gourd shaped like a long egg.

MARSHMALLOW: Candy made of sugar, corn syrup, gelatin and flavoring.

Very versatile used in cooking food and drinks.

MARZIPAN: A confection of ground almonds, sugar and egg whites shaped into attractive forms.

MASK: To cover completely with a thick sauce, mayonnaise or jelly.

MAYONNAISE: To guarantee emulsion of homemade mayonnaise, permit all ingredients to come to room temperature since emulsion will not form if eggs or oil are chilled. The secret to perfect mayonnaise is in adding one drop of oil at a time until one-half cup has been absorbed. Then add remaining oil by teaspoonfuls. Check, as you continue to beat, to be certain that each spoonful is absorbed before adding the next one. When all oil has been utilized, add one table-spoon lemon juice and one tablespoon boiling water and mix well. The juice and boiling water will lighten the mayonnaise and help it to remain stable when chilled.

To rescue mayonnaise that has separated, start again with a room-temperature egg yolk in a clean bowl. Add a dash of Dijon-style mustard and a dash of lemon juice; whip this mixture for one minute. Then beat in the separated mayonnaise, drop by drop, until you have achieved a proper emulsion. Complete your recipe from the point at which the first emulsion broke.

MEAD: A drink consisting of water and honey, fermented with malt, yeast and other ingredients.

MEASURE: To calculate accurate amounts of required ingredients.

MEASUREMENTS: The following are some of the most frequently used measurements in cooking:

3	teaspoons = 1 tablespoon
8	tablespoons = 1/2 cup
2	tablespoons liquid = 1 ounce
2	cups granulated sugar = 1 pound
3 1/2	cups powdered sugar = 1 pound
2 1/4	cups brown sugar = 1 pound
4	cups sifted all-purpose flour = 1 pound
1	pound butter = 2 cups or 4 sticks
8	ounces = 1 cup
2	cups = 1 pint
2	pints = 1 quart
4	quarts = 1 gallon

MEATBALL: Ground meat, seasoned to taste, shaped into a ball before cooking.

MELT: To dissolve with heat.

MERINGUE: A mixture of beaten egg whites and granulated sugar.

To prevent shrinkage during baking, be certain that entire surface is covered and meringue is attached securely to the edge of the dish.

For best results, allow meringues to cool in the oven.

METRICS: Let's face it folks, if you expect to shop and cook in this country, you must learn the metrics system.

The following will give you the conversion factors.

When You Know	Multiply by	To Find
MASS (weight)		
ounces	28.	grams
pounds	0.45	kilograms
MASS (weight)		
grams	0.035	ounces
kilograms	2.2	pounds
tonnes (1000 kg)	1.1	short tons

VOLUME

teaspoons	5	milliliters
tablespoons	15	milliliters
fluid ounces	30	milliliters
cups	0.24	liters
pints	0.47	liters
quarts	0.95	liters
gallons	3.8	liters

VOLUME

milliliters	0.03	fluid ounces
liters	2.1	pints
liters	1.06	quarts
liters	0.26	gallons

Here are just a few calculations done for you.

    1 teaspoon = 5 milliliters
    1 tablespoon = 15 milliliters
    1 fluid ounce = 30 milliliters
    1 cup = 240 milliliters
    1 ounce = 28 grams
    1 pound = 454 grams
    1 kilogram = 2.2 pounds

Slight adjustments have been made in these calculations to bring them to the nearest whole number.

MICROWAVE OVENS: Cooks food in one-tenth or less time than conventional methods.

Warms cooked foods without drying out.

Thaws frozen foods quickly.

Cooks small quantities of food quickly.

MILK: One-half cup evaporated milk plus one-half cup water equals one cup whole milk.

Four tablespoons nonfat dry milk plus one cup water yields one cup skim milk.

For recipes calling for sour milk, stir one tablespoon lemon juice into one cup sweet milk and let stand for a few minutes.

To scald milk, always heat in upper portion of double boiler until a row of tiny bubbles appear around the edge.

To enrich hot cocoa, malteds, milkshakes, puddings and custards, try adding three tablespoons of dry milk for each cupful of liquid.

MILLET: Small seeded cereal and forage grasses or the grain or seed from these grasses.

MINCE: To cut or chop into tiny pieces.

MINCEMEAT: A cooked mixture of minced foods and spices.

When baking mince pie, try adding one-quarter cup raisins and 2 tablespoons brandy to mincemeat before baking.

MINESTRONE: A thick Italian vegetable soup served with grated cheese.

Macaroni should not be added to minestrone soup until fifteen minutes before serving. This will prevent macaroni from being overcooked.

MINT: A strong, sweet/tangy and cool tasting herb.

To keep fresh mint fresh and crisp, wash thoroughly, shake off excess water and refrigerate in glass-covered jar.

The classic seasoning for any lamb dish or mint julep. Also delicious in custards, fruit compotes, currant jelly and beverages.

See also **HERBS & SPICES** and **SALADS.**

MIX: To combine ingredients until evenly blended, usually by stirring or beating.

MOCHA: A mixture of coffee and chocolate used as a flavoring or a beverage.

MOISTEN: To add small amount of liquid to an ingredient to make ingredient slightly wet.

MOLASSES: A thick brown syrup separated from raw sugar during stages of refinement.

MOLLUSK: Mostly shelled and aquatic invertebrate animals including snails, mussels, clams, oysters and squid.

MONOSODIUM GLUTAMATE: A flavoring agent and flavor intensifier known as MSG.

MOREL: The prized mushroom.

MORNAY: A white sauce to which cheese has been added.

MOUSSAKA: A tasty Greek dish made of layered eggplant and meat (usually lamb) casserole style.

MOUSSE: A frozen dessert made of whipped cream, egg whites, sweetening, flavoring, and occasionally with gelatin added.

MUFFINS: For lightest muffins, use pastry flour and avoid overbeating.

For best results, drop batter gently by spoonfuls into greased muffin pans, filling two-thirds full.

For fast delicious muffins, try combining one pint of softened vanilla ice cream with two cups self-rising flour and beat until smooth. Spoon into well-greased muffin pans and bake in a 425 degree oven for 20-25 minutes. (For a sweeter batter, add one tablespoon sugar.)

MULL: To make a hot beverage of cider, beer, wine or fruit juices by heating and flavoring with sugar, spices or other ingredients.

MUSCAT: A white or black wine grape with a sweet and musty flavor.

MUSCATEL: Hence a rich, sweet and fruity wine.

MUSHROOMS: For freshness and quality, select the whitest and firmest mushrooms available.

One pound serves four.

To clean mushrooms, wipe with a damp cloth. Do NOT soak in water. Mushrooms absorb water and this causes loss of taste.

Try using an egg-slicer instead of a knife for perfect mushroom slices.

See also **VEGETABLES.**

MUSSELS: A blue-shelled mollusk which clings to rocks, wharves and mud by a dark, hairy beard.

The meat is yellow with a sweet and delicate flavor.

For freshness, select mussels with tightly closed shells.

To clean, soak in cold water with one tablespoon of dry mustard for twenty minutes. Then scrub under running water until all sand is removed.

To steam, place prepared mussels in a deep kettle. Add two tablespoons of water for each dozen mussels. Cover and steam until the shells open, about three to ten minutes.

MUSTARD: *Dry Mustard* is finely ground mustard seeds.

Prepared Mustard is dry mustard that has been mixed with vinegar or water.

Herb Mustard is just that, a herb flavored mustard.

French (Dijon) and Louisiana Mustards are mild flavored prepared mustards seasoned with herbs.

English Mustard is very sharp.

MUSTARD GREENS: A peppery tasting leaf. Select fresh, young, crisp leaves with good green color.

May be eaten raw, chopped in salads, or boiled as a vegetables.

When cooking, try adding a slice of salt pork or bacon for added taste.

See also **SALADS** and **VEGETABLES**.

MUTTON: Mutton is mature lamb with flavor that is naturally a bit stronger than lamb.

This meat is frequently broiled but seldom roasted.

Mutton chops should be two-inches thick and cooked rare.

If substituted for lamb, requires ten minutes per pound extra cooking time.

NAPOLEON: A French pastry made with layers of puff paste filled with pastry cream, cut into oblong slices and sprinkled with confectioners sugar or glazed.

NECTAR: The saccharine secretion of a plant more commonly applied to any delicious tasting beverage.

NECTARINE: A fruit with a delicate flavor similar to peaches.

Select rosy, ripe nectarines since green unripened ones have a tendency to shrivel rather than ripen.

See also **FRUITS.**

NESSELRODE: The most famous nesselrode preparation is the dessert pudding (or cream pie). This is a mixture of custard enriched with heavy cream, chestnut pieces, candied orange peel, raisins, currants, cherries and flavored with maraschino liqueur.

Nesselrode may also be a game soup or a rich barley and rice soup.

Nesselrode may also be a cold dish of thrushes stuffed with truffles.

NEWBERG: A combination of heavy cream, thickened with egg yolks and flavored with wine or brandy. Generally served with fish dishes (Lobster Newburg.)

NOODLE: A pasta made of flour, water and egg yolks. The noodle is the only form of pasta that contains egg yolks.

For better taste, drain after cooking and rinse in hot water to prevent sticking.

See also **PASTA.**

NOUGAT: A confection made with roasted nuts, egg white, sugar or honey.

NUTMEG: An aromatic spice widely used in the preparation of desserts, soups, beverages and baked products.

See also **HERBS & SPICES.**

NUTS: One-pound of shelled nuts yields approximately one-half pound of nutmeats.

To preserve taste and flavor, shell nuts just before using.

Nuts slice more easily when warm and moist.

To toast nuts easily, spread out in a shallow baking pan and place in a 250 degree oven for fifteen minutes.

To chop just a few nuts at a time, place in a clean towel and roll with a rolling pin.

To prevent nuts from sticking to the blade in a food processor, sprinkle the nuts with a small amount of flour before chopping.

—

OATMEAL: To prevent lumping, sprinkle slowly into boiling salted water and stir while cooking.

To prevent sticking, cook in the top part of a double boiler over boiling water.

Long slow cooking gives regular oatmeal the best flavor.

OKRA: One pound serves four.

Select young okra with pods crisp to the touch that break easily.

For better taste, cut off stems and cut in one-half inch slices.

See also **VEGETABLES.**

OLEOMARGARINE: A smooth-textured butter substitute, low in cholesterol, used as a spread and in cooking.

OLIVES: A hard-stoned fruit used as a condiment, for seasoning and as an appetizer.

Olives are graded by size as Small, Medium, Large, Extra Large, Mammoth, Giant, Colossal and Super Colossal.

Ripe Olives are either green or black.

Dried and salt-cured olives are also known as Greek or Italian olives.

Spanish-style olives are green fermented olives.

If white scum forms on top of liquid in which bottled olives are packed, rinse olives before using. The olive will remain edible as long as it remains firm.

To make easy garlic-olives, drain liquid from green or black olives, add ten to twelve peeled cloves of garlic and cover with salad oil. Marinate in refrigerator for a few days. The oil will also make a delicious salad dressing.

Try stuffing pitted olives with toasted almonds or anchovies for fast delicious cocktail snacks.

OLIVE OIL: The best is golden in color; avoid greenish-colored oil which is of poor quality.

Keep oil away from cold temperatures; cold causes it to congeal and separate.

Try using equal amounts of olive oil and butter for smokeless sautéing.

OMELET: *See* **EGGS.**

ONIONS: Fall into the following general categories:
Globe which have a pungent flavor and are primarily used for cooking.

Granex-Grano which are somewuat flattened and
  yellow or white in color. These onions are mild in
  flavor and therefore ideal for slicing and eating
  raw.
Spanish which are also mild in flavor and generally
  larger in size. Excellent for slicing or for salads.
Bermuda which are large and flat, white or yellow in
  color. Mildly flavored and excellent for slicing and
  eating raw.
Green onions are regular onions which have been har-
  vested very young.

Select onions that are dry, unsprouted and firm to the
touch.

One pounds serves four.

For "no tears," peel under running water.

For "no tears" when chopping, sprinkle cut surfaces
with a little lemon juice.

To extract juice, cut slice from the root end and
scrape juice from the center outward. Use edge of
spoon.

To make onion rings, slice crosswise and separate the
slices into rings.

To remove odor from hands, rub with salt, lemon
juice or celery salt.

See also **VEGETABLES.**

ORANGE: Select fruit that is firm and heavy for their size.

For juicier oranges, choose smooth, thin skins and squeeze at room temperature.

To grate orange rind, rub in short strokes across small area of grater.

OREGANO: An herb closely related to marjoram. Pleasantly strong and bitter. A must in Italian dishes such as veal scallopini, pizza, pasta and sauces. Also popular in Mexican foods.

See also **HERBS and SPICES.**

OXFORD SAUCE: Usually served with cold venison or other game. Sometimes known as Cumberland Sauce.

OXTAIL: A beef tail weighing 1 1/2 to 2 1/2 pounds.

Used as the basis for Oxtail soup.

OYSTERS: *Half Shells* are the smallest oysters, excellent for eating raw.
Culls are medium size, good for eating raw and for for stewing.
Box are the largest size oysters, usually used for frying.

For freshness, select live oysters in tightly closed shells.

To shuck oysters, scrub shells and rinse in cold water. Insert point of sharp knife into hinged end of oyster. Push blade between shells until muscle at center is cut and valves start to separate. Run knife around shell, separate valves and loosen oyster from shell.

When purchasing shucked oysters, select those that are plump, with no shell particles and with clear liquid.

OYSTER PLANT: A seldom-used winter vegetable which is very ornamental.

P

PAELLA: A seasoned Spanish style rice dish usually made in a casserole. Contains poultry and shellfish.

PANBROIL: A top of the stove, dry heat method of cooking, often substituted for broiling.

Foods are cooked uncovered in a heavy skillet without adding fat or water.

For best results, preheat skillet.

PANCAKES: *See* **GRIDDLE CAKES.**

PANFRY: To fry in an uncovered skillet, on top of the stove, with very little fat.

PAPAYA: A sweet-tart, musy tasting fruit which resembles a melon.

Select ripe papaya which has yellow-orange skin and is soft to the touch.

PAPRIKA: Condiment ground from the dried ripe fruit of various mild red peppers.

PARAFFIN: A waxy substance used to coat the tops of

jars containing jams and jellies. Paraffin keeps the air out and thereby prevents spoilage.

PARBOIL: To partially cook (usually in boiling water) in preparation for further cooking.

PARCH: To dry thoroughly under dry heat.

PARE: To peel thinly with a very sharp knife.

When paring a large amount of food, try wearing a rubber office finger for protection.

PARFAIT: Cream layered with whipped cream, fruit or other sauces and arranged in a tall, narrow glass (a parfait glass).

PARMESAN: Style of food that has been prepared with a topping of parmesan cheese.

PARSLEY: Select clean, fresh-smelling, bright green bunches for top quality.

Adds flavor and color to soups.

Chopped parsley is an excellent garnish for eggs, meat, fish or salad.

To keep fresh parsley crisp, wash thoroughly, shake off excess water and refrigerate in glass-covered jar.

See also **HERBS & SPICES** and **SALADS.**

PARSNIP: Select vegetables with small or medium-sized roots. Large roots have woody cores and are tasteless.

For tastier cooked parsnips, add 1 teaspoon of sugar to the cooking water.

For added zest, try using a parsnip in chicken soup.

See also **VEGETABLES.**

PASSION FRUIT: A purple, sweet-tart, tropical fruit. It is approximately three inches long and has many seeds.

PASTA: The three basic types of pasta are spaghetti, macaroni and noodles.

Spaghetti can be round, oval, straight or wavy. Among the most popular spaghettis are vermicelli which is thin and fusilli which is twisted.

Macaroni is a pasta tube. Among the most popular would be elbow macaroni which is short and curved (like an elbow) and rigatoni which is short, wide and ridged.

Noodles are the only pasta that contain eggs. They are flat, ribbon-like strips cut in varying widths—fine, medium and broad. Lasagna and fettucini are the classics.

To properly cook one pound of pasta, boil in six quarts of water and two tablespoons of salt.

To prevent sticking, add a little olive oil to the boiling water.

Pasta that is going to be cooked beyond the boiling process should only be boiled three-quarters of the regular boiling time. This will avoid mushiness in the finished product.

When using cooked pasta in a cold salad, add the salad dressing while the pasta is still hot. This will prevent sticking and give a better flavor blend to the salad.

PASTE: A soft, smooth mixture made from nuts or other foods.

PASTEURIZE: A process of heating milk or other liquids to kill harmful bacteria.

PASTRAMI: A deli favorite which turns brisket, plate or round of beef into a highly spiced, preserved, dry-cured meat.

PASTRY: Dough used for pies, tarts, sweet and non-sweet foods served as desserts, snacks and appetizers.

Also used in baked foods such as Danish pastry and cream puffs.

PATÉ: A fish or meat paste.

Also relates to a pie with a fish or meat paste filling.

The most popular paté is paté de foie gras, which is goose liver paté.

PATTY: A small, flat cake of ground meat, fish or vegetables which is usually to be fried.

A patty is also a pastry shell filled with a creamed mixture of food.

PAVLOVA: A rich dessert consisting of a meringue topped with whipped cream and decorated with berries, passion fruit, banana slices or any combination of above fruits.

PEACH: Select peaches that are fairly firm, not bruised, with yellow or red color over entire surface.

If peaches are hard to peel, try dipping in boiling water.

See also **FRUITS.**

PEANUTS: For a change of pace, try serving ground peanuts over cooked vegetables or pasta. You will find a delicious texture contrast.

See also **NUTS.**

PEAR: Select those with thin skins, good color for their variety and unblemished.

Ripe and ready to eat when they yield slightly to moderate pressure.

For best results, always ripen pears at room temperature.

See also **FRUITS.**

PEAS: For sweetness, select pods that are well-filled but not bulging. Should also have a velvety texture.

One pound in shell yields approximately one cup shelled.

Try adding sweet fresh green peas to a salad.

See also **VEGETABLES.**

PECANS: To shell easily, pour boiling water over pecans and allow them to cool. Then just crush from end to end.

See also **NUTS.**

PECTIN: A substance which forms a jelly when it is combined with sugar and acid. It is used in the making of jams and jellies.

PEEL: To remove the outer peel, skin or rind of food.

PEPPERS: Fresh *red* or *green* peppers should have a glossy sheen, be heavy for their size and have firm walls and sides.

For better tasting stuffed peppers, tenderize before stuffing and baking by cooking in boiling salted water for five minutes.

Hot *red* or *green chili* peppers are used mainly as a seasoning. Use sparingly or beware!

See also **VEGETABLES.**

PEPPER, GROUND: For peak flavor, serve pepper in a pepper mill. Freshly ground pepper enhances all foods it is used on.

Use white pepper where black specs are not desired (mashed potatoes, white sauces, clear soups, etc.).

Cayenne pepper is a very strong red pepper. Use sparingly but a pinch in all souffles makes a surprising difference.

See also **HERBS & SPICES.**

PEPPERCORN: The dried berry of the black pepper plant which is ground in a pepper mill.

See also **HERBS & SPICES.**

PEPPERONE: A highly spiced dry sausage of Italian origin.

PERCH: A mild fish with firm white coarse flesh and a delicate flavor.

Select perch with firm flesh, clear full eyes, red gills and a shiny skin.

Cook over low heat for the shortest possible time to keep perch moist and tender.

Perch fillets are best for poaching.

Whole perch is best for steaming.

Cut fillets are best for deep frying.

Small whole perch are best for sautéing.

See also **FISH.**

PERSIMMON: Select plump, smooth fruit with a glossy skin and stem cap attached.

Ripens best in a cool, dark, dry place. When ripe looks somewhat like a tomato and is reddish-orange in color.

For best flavor chill before serving.

Properly eaten with a spoon.

PETITE MARMITE: A French meal-in-one soup.

PETITS FOURS: Small cakes of assorted shapes and fillings; very elegantly frosted and decorated.

PFEFFERNEUSSE: A traditional, spicy Christmas cookie, sprinkled with confectioner's sugar.

PICCALILLI: A pickle relish.

PICKLES: When buying deli-barrel pickles, store them in well-sealed jars with either plastic or glass tops rather than metal lids. This will avoid corrosion and keep your pickles fresh longer.

PICKLING: A process whereby food is preserved in salt, an acid liquid such as vinegar, or sugar, or any combination of the three. May be pickled with or without spices.

PIE: For a richer chiffon pie, fold one cup whipped cream into the filling before spooning into pie shell.

Tastiest pumpkin pies should always contain one-half teaspoon cloves and one-half teaspoon nutmeg in filling.

For a softer filling in lemon meringue pie, use one less egg yolk.

For a softer filling in rhubarb pie, omit eggs.

PIE CRUST: Too much flour makes crust tough.

Too much shortening makes crust dry and crumbly.

Too much liquid makes crust heavy and soggy.

If crust is to be baked with filling, do not prick.

If crust only is to be baked, prick bottom and sides well before baking to permit air to escape.

Crust will brown easier either in a glass baking dish or a pie tin that has grown dark from use rather than in a new tin or aluminum pan.

To prevent soggy bottom crusts in filled pies, brush crust lightly with an egg white before filling.

For a glossy top crust, brush with mixture of one egg and one tablespoon of water before baking.

For even color and texture, top crust may be brushed with milk.

For a richer crumb-pie shell, add one cup chopped nut meats.

For a nice change, make a chocolate crumb pie shell by crushing chocolate wafers.

One cup grated cheese sprinkled on the top crust of any fruit pie adds extra flavor and zest.

PIKE: Select fish with firm flesh, clear full eyes, red gills and a shiny skin.

A lean fish, delicious when steamed, poached, pan fried or baked.

To keep moist and tender, cook over low heat for the shortest possible time.

See also **FISH.**

PILAF: A well seasoned, long-grained rice dish sautéed in oil or butter; then boiled in broth. Meat, fish, seafood, vegetables, herbs or spices may be included.

PIMENTO: Sweet red peppers that have been preserved in oil. Delicious in salads and a favorite garnish because of their bright red coloring.

PINCH: A measurement of the tiniest amount. Generally what amount may be picked up between the tip of the index finger and the thumb.

PINEAPPLE: Select fruit heavy for its size, slightly soft to the touch and with a fruity aroma.

A medium-sized pineapple yields three cups of diced fruit.

For peak taste, chill one hour before serving.

PIT: To remove pits or seeds from any food that requires pitting.

PIZZA: A flat yeast dough covered with tomato sauce, cheese, peppers, mushrooms, sausage, anchovies, or any desired combination of food.

PLANK: To broil and serve meat or fish on a board made for that purpose.

PLUM: Select fruit that is deep colored for its variety and slightly soft to the touch.

Ripen plums at room temperature.

See also **FRUIT.**

PLUM PUDDING: A traditional suet pudding that may be either steamed or boiled. It is served as a dessert with sauce.

POACH: To cook slowly in simmering water (not boiling) or in a receptacle put over simmering water.

POI: The staple food of Hawaii made from the root of the taro plant.

POLENTA: The Italian term for any dish made with cornmeal mush.

POMEGRANATE: Select those that are heavy for their size, with a thin skin and a very bright color.

For peak flavor, chill, cut in half, and serve with spoon.

Pomegranate seeds add zest to fruit salad.

Also known as Chinese apples.

POPOVER: A quick bread made from an egg rich batter.

To reheat popovers, place in a dampened paper bag for five minutes in a 425 degree oven.

POPPY SEEDS: Crunchy and nutlike in flavor, each ripe pod holds hundreds of tiny seeds.

Use in breads, salads, and bland dishes like cabbage and noodles.

PORK: The flesh of domestic swine and a very good source of high quality protein.

When purchasing fresh pork look for flesh that is grayish-pink, firm and finely grained.

Should always be thoroughly cooked to kill any trichinae organisms present. In a 325 degree oven, cook a small roast 45 minutes per pound and a large roast 35 minutes per pound.

The choice pork roasts are the rib, loin and shoulder.

When preparing roast crown of pork, allow two chops per person.

Rib, loin or shoulder pork chops are at their best when cut one-inch thick.

The suggested amount to buy per serving is one-third pound for boneless cuts, one-half pound for partially boned cuts and one pound for boney cuts.

Timetables for cooking pork.

FOR BRAISING

Kind and cut of meat	Approximate ready-to-cook weight or thickness	Approximate total cooking time
		Hours
Chops.....................1/2 to 1 inch......		3/4 to 1
Spareribs................. 2 to 3 pounds......		1 1/2 to 2 1/2

FOR BROILING

Kind and cut of meat	Approximate thickness	Degree of doneness	Approximate total cooking time[1]
	Inches		*Minutes*
Cured ham slices.....	3/4	Well done...	13 to 14
(Cook-before-eating)	1	Well done...	18 to 20

[1]*Meat at refrigerator temperature at start of broiling.*

Kind and cut of meat	Ready-to-cook weight	Approximate roasting time at 325° F.	Internal temperature of meat when done
	Pounds	*Hours*	*°F.*
PORK, FRESH			
Loin, center cut.......	3 to 5	2 to 3 1/2	170
Shoulder, picnic.......	5 to 8	3 to 4	170
Ham, whole..........	12 to 16	5 1/2 to 6	170
Ham, boneless, rolled..	10 to 14	4 2/3 to 5 1/2	170
Spareribs.............	3 to 4	2	....
PORK, CURED			
Cook-before-eating:			
Ham, whole........	10 to 14	3 1/2 to 4 1/4	160
Ham, half..........	5 to 7	2 to 2 1/2	160
Picnic shoulder......	6	3 1/2	170
Fully cooked:[1]			
Ham, whole........	12 to 16	3 1/2 to 4	140
Ham, half..........	5 to 7	2	140

[1]*Meat at refrigerator temperature at start of roasting.*

Pork is marinated for flavor rather than for tenderness, since the pork fat makes the pork naturally more tender.

Try a dash of poultry seasoning to improve flavor.

Fresh or cooked pork may be kept up to three months in the freezer.

A tart fruit accompaniement enhances the flavor of pork.

PORRIDGE: A thickened soup-like substance made by boiling a grain or other food in water or milk.

POTATO: Select those that are firm, smooth, free from blemishes and are reasonably clean. Avoid potatoes with green skins as they have a tendency to be bitter.

To cook old potatoes, put them in cold water and bring to a boil.

To cook new potatoes, plunge them into already boiling water and cook until just soft for best results.

Idaho potatoes are the best tasting for baking.

To reheat a leftover baked potato or sweet potato, dip in hot water and simply rebake for ten minutes or so in a 450 degree oven.

See also **VEGETABLES.**

POT-AU-FEU: French version of a boiled dinner.

POTPOURRI: A mixture of spices and dried flower petals used to fragrance a room.

POT ROASTING: Another name for braising when applied to cooking of meat.

POULTRY: Domesticated birds bred and raised for use as human feed. The most popular are chickens, ducks, turkeys, rock cornish hens.

A rule of thumb for purchasing poultry is choose a wide bodied, round breasted, short legged bird. The skin should be free of bruises and look clean.

Poultry rule of thumb serving portions are:

	Servings per pound[1]
Chicken	2 or 3
Turkey	2 or 3
Duck and goose	2

[1]Three ounces of cooked lean poultry per serving.

Remove poultry from the refrigerator one hour before cooking. Poultry cooks evenly when started at room temperature. BUT, do not allow to stand at room temperature longer than two hours as bacteria will start to develop.

When preparing poultry, run cold water through or over the bird, never soak it in water. Water saps the natural flavor from poultry.

Poultry should be kept frozen until ready to use, allow enough time for thawing before cooking. Broiler-fryers require twelve to twenty-four hours to thaw in refrigerator and larger birds proportionately more time.

Whenever possible, season poultry the day before cooking for better taste.

Before freezing poultry parts, wrap tightly in freezer paper, making sure pieces fit closely together to avoid air spaces which promote spoilage in the freezer.

Frozen cooked poultry retains its quality for up to three months.

Before refrigerating or freezing, remove any dressing from stuffed birds to prevent bacterial growth. Store dressing separately.

When baking poultry, you will have juicier meat and less shrinkage if you use a constant low heat of 325 degrees. Increase oven temperature to 425 degrees for last fifteen minutes of cooking time, breast side up, for added color and crisper skin.

Roasting guide for poultry:

Kind of poultry	Ready-to-cook weight[1]	Approximate roasting time at 325° F. for stuffed poultry[2]	Internal temperature of poultry when done
	Pounds	*Hours*	*° F.*
Chickens............	1 1/2 to 2 1/2	1 to 2....	
(Broilers, fryers, or roasters)	2 1/2 to 4 1/2	2 to 3 1/2	
Ducks..............	4 to 6....	2 to 3....	
Geese..............	6 to 8....	3 to 3 1/2	
	8 to 12...	3 1/2 to 4 1/2	
Turkeys............	6 to 8....	3 to 3 1/2	
	8 to 12...	3 1/2 to 4 1/2	180 to 185
	12 to 16...	4 1/2 to 5 1/2	in center of
	16 to 20...	5 1/2 to 6 1/2	inner thigh
	20 to 24...	6 1/2 to 7....	muscle.

[1] Weight of giblets and neck included.
[2] Unstuffed poultry may take slightly less time than stuffed poultry. Cooking time is based on chilled poultry or poultry that has just been thawed—temperature not above 40° F. Frozen unstuffed poultry will take longer. Do not use this roasting guide for frozen commercially stuffed poultry; follow package directions.

When roasting, bird is properly done when drumstick moves up and down easily. Continue cooking until this occurs or bird will be undercooked.

To test broiled poultry for doneness, prick with a skewer. If juice is red, additional broiling is required.

When sauteéing, dry bird thoroughly before starting cooking process or it will not brown properly.

PRALINE: A crisp candy made of pecans, almonds or other nuts, browned in boiling sugar.

PREHEAT: To heat to a desired temperature *before* cooking food.

PRESSURE COOKER: A very handy kitchen appliance for quick cooking. Foods cook in a fraction of the time necessary by conventional methods on or in a stove.

PROSCIUTTO: Delectable, thinly-sliced Italian ham.

PUDDING: A variety of baked, boiled or steamed soft foods with a custardy texture. May be served hot or cold as a dessert or main dish.

When making snow puddings, combine all ingredients at high speed and then whip until texture holds its shape.

PUFF: A light pastry often made hollow so that it can be filled. (Cream puffs, eclairs, etc.)

PUMPKIN: Select pumpkin with a firm rind and a bright orange color.

Three pounds of fresh pumpkin yields about three cups cooked and mashed pumpkin.

Small pumpkins are more tender for cooking purposes.

PUNCH: A beverage served from a large bowl into small cups.

Alcoholic punch may be served either hot or cold.

Fruit juice punches are always served ice cold.

PUREE: Food prepared by straining the boiled pulp through a sieve.

Also a thick soup with puree in it.

QUAIL: A small game bird that looks like a small, plump chicken with white meat and flesh of a delicate flavor.

Allow one quail per serving.

Young quail may be panfried, panbroiled, broiled or roasted.

Older birds are tough and should be braised with a marinade.

QUENELLE: A dumpling made with pressed fish or meat. Small ones are used as a garnish. Large ones are served as a separate dish.

QUICHE: One nine-inch quiche yields eight generous servings or twelve medium servings.

Do not overbake or the quiche will be watery in the middle.

For better taste, serve warm, not piping hot.

Never freeze quiche, creamy texture will be destroyed.

For a quick quiche crust, press a thin layer of leftover spaghetti on bottom and sides of a buttered quiche pan. Pour in any desired quiche mixture and bake as usual. Crust browns beautifully.

QUINCE: Select fruit that is deep yellow in color.

Quinces are too tart to eat raw but are delicious for marinade, jelly, jam and preserves.

R

RADISH: Select firm, medium-sized, well-formed radishes. Avoid oversized ones as they tend to be pithy.

For better taste, crisp in ice water before serving.

Make beautiful garnishes when shaped into roses or tulips.

See also **VEGETABLES.**

RAGOUT: A stew made from meat, poultry or fish that has cooked in thick rich sauces, with or without vegetables.

RAISE: A method of making food light and porous by the action of yeast.

RAISIN: A dried grape. Available in both black and white raisins.

RAMEKIN: An individual baking dish, usually with one lip, in which food is baked and served.

RAMEQUIN: A cheese tart.

RAREBIT: A popular melted cheese dish also known as Welsh rarebit, or rabbit.

RASPBERRIES: Select those that are plump, dry, solid and of good color. Raspberries with clinging caps may be underripe.

Clean just before using for peak taste.

To clean, wash gently under slow-running water. Do not soak, water hastens spoilage.

See also **FRUIT.**

RATATOUILLE: A French stew or casserole containing eggplant, zucchini, tomato and green pepper. Can be served warm or cold.

RAVIOLI: Shells of noodle dough filled with meat, chicken, cheese, spinach, or any desired filling.

When preparing, moisten the edges of the filled dough with water and press securely together. This will prevent ravioli from opening during cooking.

Cooked ravioli should be removed from liquid with slotted spoon for best results.

RECIPE: A formula for preparing food. Should be followed as accurately as possible.

RECONSTITUTE: To restore concentrated food, such as frozen orange juice or dry milk, to its original state, usually by adding water.

REDUCE: To cook a liquid until part is cooked away

so that the flavor will be compressed and the portion that remains will be of a thicker consistency.

REHYDRATE: To soak or cook dried foods to restore the water lost in drying.

RELISHES: Those such as celery, carrots, scallions, pickles and olives may be left on the table during dinner since they are always served cold from a platter.

Cranberry sauce, preserves and other main course accompaniments are also considered popular relishes.

REMOLADE: A spicy sauce made with the yolks of hard-cooked eggs, vinegar, oil, and served with cold dishes or as a salad dressing.

RENDER: To melt fat trimmed from meat or poultry by heating slowing at a low temperature.

RHUBARB: Select firm young stalks with fresh-looking leaves for tenderness.

One pound yields about two cups, cooked.

Rhubarb adds zest to any cooked fruit compote.

See also **FRUIT.**

RICE: One cup of raw rice makes approximately three cups, cooked.

To prevent sticking, add one tablespoon of margarine before boiling.

To avoid blackening of aluminum pot when cooking rice, add one-quarter teaspoon of vinegar or lemon juice while cooking.

White, brown or wild rice may be kept warm for a short time over hot water in a double boiler.

In damp weather, try adding a few grains of rice to salt shakers for easing pouring.

RICE: To reduce food to ricelike pellets by pressing through a sievelike utensil (riced potatoes).

RISSOLE: A baked or fried pastry filled with meat, fish or fruit.

Also to sear food with a protective covering.

ROAST: To cook by dry heat, usually in an oven.

ROASTER: Chicken used for roasting, weighing from 2 1/2 to 5 pounds.

See also **POULTRY.**

ROCK CORNISH HENS: Tasty fowl bred specifically for good eating. Maximum weight is up to two pounds. Used for roasting, broiling and baking.

See also **POULTRY.**

ROE: Eggs of fish.

ROSEMARY: An herb curved like a pine needle with a fresh sweet taste. Excellent with roast beef, fish, poultry and lamb.

See also **HERBS & SPICES.**

ROTISSERIE: An appliance used to cook foods by rotating them in front of or over a source of heat; more simply—any turning spit.

ROUX: A fat and starch base used for thickening sauces or soups.

ROSETTE: A decoratively shaped cake fried in deep fat. Lighter in texture than a doughut.

ROSEWATER: Flavoring distilled from rose petals.

RUM: An alcoholic beverage distilled from fermented products of the sugar cane.

A widely used flavoring used in confections and baked goods.

RUTABAGA: Select smooth, firm rutabaga that are heavy for their size.

Use a stiff brush to remove wax coating or peel well before cooking.

Cook as you would turnips.

To improve taste, add a teaspoon of sugar to the water before cooking.

See also **VEGETABLES**.

SABAYON: The French name for Italian Zabaglione, a sherry or wine-flavored custard.

SAGE: An herb commonly used in poultry stuffing. Also tasty with fish, salads and pork.

See also **HERBS & SPICES.**

SAFFRON: The world's most costly spice. It requires 75,000 blossoms from a particular crocus plant to make just one pound.

Used for flavoring and coloring of only special foods such as yellow rice.

See also **HERBS & SPICES.**

SAKE: The traditional alcoholic drink of Japan, made from fermented rice.

SALADS: Add color, flavor and texture to meals. Salads may be presented as an appetizer, main course, an accompaniment to a main course or a dessert. In addition to all this versatility they are full of health-giving vitamins and minerals.

Salad-making is an art. To achieve the very best results make sure the ingredients are fresh, cold, crisp and dry.

The proper blending of assorted salad leaves is just as important as the dressing that goes with it. Mix and match for super results. For example, head lettuce tastes bland, watercress sweet, collards cabbagy, escarole sharp and mustard greens are bitter.

Serve a fruit salad as an appetizer, a light salad with a heavy meal, a tart salad with fish andd a hearty salad as a main course.

To prepare green leaves for a salad, first wash them in lukewarm water and then cold. Place the leaves in a plastic bag and seal it. Punch a tiny hole in the bag and refrigerate. The water will evaporate and leaves will remain fresh and crisp for a longer period of time. Keep all salad greens well-chilled until ready to serve.

Never cut salad greens with a knife. Always tear into pieces to prevent edges from browning.

Leave edible peel on fruit or vegetables for salads whenever possible but be sure to scrub them with a stiff brush. Important vitamins are saved this way.

For perfect results with oil and vinegar salad dressing, pour vinegar over greens first, then the oil. If reversed, the oil will coat the greens and prevent vinegar from penetrating.

Try lemon juice instead of vinegar in salad dressing for a nice change.

Want more change? Rub inside of salad bowl with cut cloves of shallots before adding salad greens.

Never slice tomatoes directly into a salad. They contain acid and water and will dilute the dressing. Arrange on top of salad until ready to serve.

For easier serving, use a scissor-like serving implement.

For a different look, try serving salad in a soup tureen instead of a salad bowl.

Never wash wooden salad bowls. Just rinse and wipe dry.

SALLY LUNN: A southern bread baked in muffin pans.

SALMON: For uncleaned fresh fish, allow one pound per serving.

For cleaned fresh fish, allow one-half pound per serving.

To prevent breakage during steaming, wrap fish in a piece of cheesecloth before starting to steam. This will guarantee easy removal.

For canned salmon, excess oil may be removed by rinsing with hot water.

Smoked salmon is known as lox, a delicacy.

See also **FISH** and **SMOKED FISH.**

SALT PORK: The cured side of a hog.

SASSAFRA: A thickening and seasoning agent which forms the base of gumbo.

SAUCE: A liquid accompaniment to food.

Canned soups may be used as an excellent base for many sauces.

SAUERBRATEN: Of German origin, beef or pork dish marinated in vinegar before cooking.

SAUSAGE: All fresh and smoked pork sausages require cooking before eating.

Dry sausages require no cooking.

To maintain flavor, dry sausage must be refrigerated once casing is opened.

When frying tiny sausages, fasten four or five in a row with wooden picks. You can then turn several at a time for even browning.

SAUTÉ: To fry quickly and turn frequently in little fat.

SAVORY: An herb of the mint family with an aromatic flavor.

May be used alone or combined with other herbs to

flavor meats, chicken, eggs, salads, sauces and meat dressings.

See also **HERBS & SPICES.**

SCALD: To heat liquid to just below the boiling point.

SCALDING: Pretreatment of vegetables with boiling water before freezing.

SCALLOPING: Baking a casserole that contains pieces of food which have been arranged in alternate layers with a sauce or other liquid. Usually contains a crumb topping.

SCALLOPS: A white, meaty shellfish.

Usually served fried but may also be prepared broiled or stewed and served in a cream sauce.

SCALOPPINE: A style of cooking whereby slices of meat (usually veal) and fish have been flattened and fried in butter or oil.

To prevent butter from burning, try mixing with equal parts of oil.

SCHNITZEL: The German term for veal cutlet.

SCONE: A biscuitlike tea cake.

May be either cooked on a griddle or baked in oven.

SCORE: To cut narrow grooves or gashes in the outer surfaces of meats. This allows fat to drain properly.

SCRAMBLE: A style of preparing food by stirring it. Usually applied to eggs which are first beaten lightly with a fork.

SCRAPPLE: A solid mush made from the by-products of hog butchering.

SCUNGILLI: The Italian word for conch, a large shellfish encased in a spiral shell.

Scungilli is prepared by cutting the conch meat into pieces, sautéing, and serving with scrambled eggs or as an omelet filling.

SEAR: To brown the surface of meat quickly in a skillet by intense heat.

SEASON: To make foods tastier by the addition of herbs or spices, condiments, sauces or flavoring or any combination thereof.

SEMOLINA: The medium-sized particles of ground grains of wheat.

SESAME SEEDS: A spice with a nutlike flavor.

May be used in almost any dish calling for almonds and in many breads and confections.

Try sprinkling over cold cooked spinach.

See also **HERBS & SPICES.**

SET: To become solid or fixed when applied to foods such as gelatins or aspics.

SHALLOTS: A mild flavored relative of the onion.

Shallots fall into the green onion category and are used primarily when a subtle onion flavor is desired.

See also **VEGETABLES.**

SHERBET: A frozen dessert made from fruit juice or puree with the addition of milk and other ingredients.

SHIRR: To bake with crumbs in small buttered dishes. Generally refers to eggs.

SHRED: To cut with a knife or shredder into thin narrow strips.

SHRIMP: A popular shellfish which should be firm to the touch and have a fresh sweet odor when purchased.

Four size grades:
Jumbo—approximately twenty per pound.
Large—approximately twenty-three per pound.
Medium—approximately thirty per pound.
Small—thirty-five and more per pound.

To devein shrimp, cut about an eighth of an inch deep along the outside curve and lift out black vein while washing shrimp under cold water.

To butterfly shrimp, cut *almost* into halves and flatten.

To elminate tinny taste from canned shrimp, soak them in two tablespoons of vinegar and a little sherry for about twenty minutes.

SHUCK: To remove an outer covering like a husk or shell. Corn is shucked by stripping their husks; oysters are shucked by removing their shells.

SIFT: To finely texture dry ingredients, such as flour, by putting through a sifter.

SIMMER: To cook in liquid just below the boiling point at temperatures from 185 F. to 210 F. Bubbles will form slowly and break below the surface.

SKEWERS: Long wooden or metal pins used to keep food in position during cooking.

SLOW COOKER: A simmering process cooking appliance wherein foods may be prepared over a long period of time unattended.

This method usually requires more seasoning. Taste before serving.

For carefree buffet entertaining, prepare hot meats, hot soups, or hot drinks in slow cookers early in the day and serve right from the crockery pots for easy dining.

Try serving hot appetizers in a slow cooker. It holds large quantities of food and will eliminate running back and forth for refills.

Slow cookers will also give perfect consistency and temperature to bean dip or hot cheese.

SMOKED FISH: Fish is smoked for flavor rather than as a preservative. This puts all smoked fishes in the delicacy class and they are generally expensive.

Smoked fish should not be kept refrigerated for longer than one week.

Some of the more popular varieties are:
Lox—smoked salmon, the belly is most choice.
Sable—smoked coalfish with oyster-white meat.
Whitefish—smoked whitefish belonging to the salmon family.
Carp—smoked carp.
Sturgeon—smoked sturgeon.
Bloater—smoked mackerel.
Baked salmon—don't be misled, this salmon is baked by smoke and falls in the smoked fish category.
Kippers—smoked herring.

Smoked fish is delicious when served in small quantities as an appetizer.

Some varieties of smoked fish make delicious meals when combined with a cold salad.

If you find the taste of smoked herrings too strong, try soaking them in half milk/half water for several hours before serving.

SOUFFLE: *See* **EGGS.**

SOUFFLE DISH: A round, fluted, fireproof, china dish with straight sides.

6 1/2 inch size used for three eggs.

SOUP: May be served piping hot or icy cold but either way, soup is highly nutritious and an important part of the meal to many people.

There are innumerable ways to prepare soup and innumerable varieties to please every taste. Generally, a clear broth or consomme is used as an appetizer. For a meal in itself try one of the stick-to-the-ribs varieties. Whatever kind pleases your palate can be a most satisfying snack.

All soups should be seasoned lightly in the beginning and additional seasoning added before serving, if needed.

Oops! Too salty, add a few slices of raw, peeled potato to absorb the salt.

To remove fine sediment from broths, run liquid through a paper coffee filter for perfect results.

To remove fat from hot soup float a lettuce leaf on top to absorb the fat.

If soup is to be used later, chill, skim fat off the top and then reheat.

To obtain full flavor from soups, simmer in covered

pots. Fast cooking retards flavor and causes evaporation.

Homemade soup always tastes better when aged at least a day.

Freeze small portions of leftover meats, fish or vegetables to add to soup as needed.

Added taste and color will be given to chicken soup by the addition of a large, washed, whole onion. Remove after cooking as it may overflavor soup if left in.

The trick in making great pea soup is to leave enough meat on the ham bone.

Feeling daring, try adding a few cubes of salami to pea soup for added zest.

If homemade chicken soup cooks down too far, add a can of ready to serve chicken consomme instead of water for truer flavor.

Soup may be refrigerated for a few weeks. BUT, to avoid souring, take it out of refrigerator and bring to a vigorous boil every two days.

Canned soups should be simmered over low heat for a few extra minutes to bring out full flavor.

Some canned soups do not require the addition of liquids. Read labels carefully.

Canned soups are good bases for sauces and gravies.

Wine added to soup can be like a marriage made in heaven. However, wine should only be added to hot soup shortly before it is to be served. Do not boil soup after adding the wine as it will cause soup to sour. After adding wine, heat slowly and serve immediately.

Try adding one-quarter cup of dry cherry or madeira to chicken soup.

Add one-half cup of dry red table wine to one quart of any beef soup.

Add one-quarter dry white table wine to one quart clam chowder or lobster bisque.

Hot soups containing wine cannot be stored for future use as the reheating process will sour the soup.

Try serving chilled soup in a tall jug or large cookie jar for summer outdoor entertaining. It can easily be served in paper cups for a fun occasion.

SPARERIBS: Allow one pound per person.

See also **PORK.**

SPATULA: A broad flexible utensil, available in various sizes, with or without slots.

Indispensable for manipulating fried foods or for icing cakes.

SPICES: *See* **HERBS & SPICES.**

SPINACH: Select leaves that are young, tender, and free from blemishes.

One pound serves four.

For easier cleaning, wash under running water to remove sand or grit.

Spinach to be used in salads should be washed, drained and dried with paper towels so that leaves will absorb dressing properly.

See also **VEGETABLES** and **SALADS.**

SPREADS: Spreads are firmer than dips.

They should be served with knives for easy convenience.

Assorted crackers complete the attractive spread serving.

SQUASH: *Acorn* squash should be selected with very few specks of orange since orange is a sign of over-ripeness.

Remove wax coating with a vegetable brush before cooking.

Allow one-half acorn squash per serving.

Three pounds will equal approximately three cups mashed.

For easier cutting, cut lengthwise between ribs.

Season and serve as you would sweet potatoes or yams.

For a delightful surprise, try substituting mashed acorn squash for the pie filling in pumpkin pie.

Butternut squash should be smooth-skinned with hard, tough rinds.

Use a potato peeler for easier peeling being sure to remove the underlayer of green which has a bitter taste.

For easier handling, scoop out seeds and stringy portions before slicing or cubing.

Hubbard squash should have a hard-warted rind which is free from blemishes.

For easier cutting use a large knife and a mallet.

For added zest, try using a little honey in any mashed squash.

See also **VEGETABLES.**

STALK: An individual piece, such as a stalk of celery or a stalk of rhubarb.

STEAK: *See* **BEEF.**

STEAM: To cook in steam, with or without pressure. Food may be steamed in a covered container on a rack or in a perforated pan over boiling water.

STEAMBAKE: To cook in oven in a pan set over a container of hot water.

STEEP: To allow a substance to stand in liquid below the boiling point in order to extract flavor, color or other components.

STEW: To cook in liquid, just below the boiling point.

STEWING CHICKEN: Weighs between 2 1/2 to 5 pounds and is used for stewing or braising.

See also **POULTRY.**

STOCK: Water in which fish, meat, poultry or any foods have been cooked and is to be used as a base for soups or gravies.

STRAWBERRIES: Select those that are plump, solid, bright in color, with caps attached. No caps indicates berries are overripe.

For best results, wash gently just before using.

Never remove stems until after washing.

Do not soak in water. Strawberries are very perishable and water hastens spoilage.

STUFF: To fill cavity with any desired dressing before cooking.

STUFFING: *See* **DRESSING.**

SUBSTITUTIONS: 2 teaspoons rice flour = 1 3/4 tablespoons flour (for thickening).

1 tablespoon cornstarch (for thickening) = 2 tablespoons flour.

1 tablespoon arrowroot = 2 tablespoons Four (for thickening).

1 cup sifted all-purpose flour = 1 cup plus 2 tablespoons sifted cake flour.

1 cup cake flour = 7/8 cup all-purpose flour for baking.

1 teaspoon baking powder = 1/4 teaspoon baking soda plus 1/2 teaspoon cream of tartar.

1 cup bread crumbs = 3/4 cup cracker crumbs.

1 whole egg = 2 egg yolks OR 2 tablespoons dried whole eggs plus 2 1/2 tablespoons water.

1 cup butter = 1 cup shortening plus 1/2 teaspoon salt OR 7/8 cup lard.

1 cup heavy sour cream = 1/3 cup butter and 2/3 cup milk in any sour-milk recipe.

1 cup thin sour cream = 3 tablespoons butter and 3/4 cup milk in any sour-milk recipe.

1 cup whole milk = 1/2 cup evaporated milk plus 1/2 cup water.

1 cup sour milk = 1 cup sweet milk into which 1 tablespoon vinegar or lemon juice has been mixed OR 1 cup buttermilk.

1 cup sweet milk = 1 cup sour milk or buttermilk plus 1/2 teaspoon baking soda.

1 cup honey = 1 cup molasses.

1 square chocolate (ounce) = 3 to 4 tablespoons dry cocoa plus 1/2 tablespoon fat.

SUGAR: One pound granulated sugar yields 2 1/4 cups.

For added zing, place slices of lemon, lime or orange in jar of granulated sugar and cover. Set aside until citrus flavor is absorbed by sugar. Now try using this citrus sugar in tea or lemonade. Yummy!

See also **CONFECTIONERS SUGAR** and **BROWN SUGAR.**

SWEET POTATO: *See* **YAM.**

TACO: A folded tortilla stuffed with spiced chopped meat or chicken. Tomatoes, shredded lettuce and cheese tops it off. Served hot.

TAMALE: A Mexican food consisting of a cornmeal dough that is stuffed with highly seasoned ground meat, cheese or other filling, and then steamed in corn husks.

TARRAGON: An herb whose dried leaves and flowering tops have a faintly aniselike flavor.

Used for flavoring vinegar, seafood and *over*-broiled chicken.

See also **HERBS & SPICES**.

TART: A pastry filled with fruit, jam, custard, eggs, meat, cheese or any desired fillings.

TEA: For peak taste in brewing tea, use a china or glass teapot. Metal pots give tea a metallic taste.

For perfectly brewed tea, never boil tea leaves. Just pour boiling water over the leaves and steep.

Very hard water causes cloudy tea. Use bottled water if available.

For added flavor, try storing teabags in airtight containers together with cinnamon sticks, cloves or vanilla beans.

Instant tea is excellent for making iced tea as it dissolves in cold water very quickly.

For undiluted iced tea, use tea-flavored cubes that have been frozen for just this purpose.

For tastier and attractive tea drinks, try adding a clove-studded lemon slice.

TETRAZZINE: Of Italian origin consisting of cooked chicken and spaghetti baked in a rich cream sauce.

THICKEN: A process to make a liquid food thicker or denser in consistency.

THYME: An aromatic and pungent herb. The finest herb for use with fish but also goes well with tomatoes and poultry dressings.

See also **HERBS & SPICES.**

TIDBITS: Any appetizer that may be picked up with fingers, toothpick or cocktail fork.

Nuts, raisins, figs and fresh sliced fruit are delicious fast tidbits.

For an unusual and beautiful table centerpiece, try studding a fresh pineapple with tidbits of cold cuts and bits of cheese. Colored toothpicks would also add to the excitement.

TIMBALE: A custard-like mixture baked in molds or custard cups which are then unmolded and served either plain or with a sauce.

TINT: To add a coloring substance to foods to intensify their palate appeal.

TOMATOES: Select tomatoes that are plump, firm and uniformly pink, red, or yellow, according to their variety.

For easy peeling, dip in boiling water and then in cold water to chill. Skin will slip off.

When baking, use those of uniform size for even cooking.

Do not cook tomatoes in metal pots. Their acid content will give them a metallic taste.

Never slice tomatoes directly into a salad. They contain acid and water which will dilute the salad dressing. Arrange on top of salad until ready to serve.

See also **SALADS** and **VEGETABLES.**

TORTILLA: A thin, round unleavened cake prepared from corn and then baked.

TRUFFLE: A potato-shaped fungus that grows underground and is valued as a table delicacy.

TRUSS: To fasten together with string or skewers.

TUREEN: A deep bowl from which foods (soup) are served *at* the table.

TURKEY: The ideal size for a good turkey is from ten to twelve pounds.

Frozen turkeys should be thawed in the refrigerator. Allow twenty-four hours for each six pounds of turkey.

A thawed, fresh, ready-to-cook turkey may be kept refrigerated for one to two days.

The favorite method for cooking a turkey is to roast it, allowing twenty minutes per pound in a 325 degree oven.

As a rule of thumb, bland stuffings like bread or oyster are best for the turkey.

For easier carving, let stand twenty minutes after roasting.

See also **POULTRY.**

TURMERIC: A spice from a plant in the ginger family.

See also **HERBS & SPICES.**

TURNIPS: Select clean turnips with firm roots.

One pounds serves three.

Sliced raw and thin, they add a crunchy tang to salad.

See also **VEGETABLES.**

UNTIL SET: A period of time until a liquid becomes firm, usually applied to a gelatine mixture.

UPSIDE-DOWN CAKE: Cake baked by placing topping in bottom of pan and the batter on top of that. When cake is inverted, topping becomes the upper portion of cake. Cake therefore has baked upside-down.

For a nice change, try baking individual upside-down cakes in custard cups.

VEAL: Veal is young beef, four to fourteen weeks of age. Actually, most of the meat sold is calf from animals fourteen weeks to one year of age.

The color of veal varies with the age of the animal, becoming redder with increasing age.

The texture of veal should be fine and velvety. Young milk-fed veal will have a greyish-pink color and no marbling.

On the average, a six pound veal roast will serve eight.

Roasts will be kept juicy by rubbing a good coating of fat into its surface. This will also give roast a beautiful brown color when cooked.

For best results, veal roasts should be cooked uncovered for thirty minutes to the pound in a 325 degree oven.

Veal roasts should be well done for proper tenderness. Most veal cuts have a large amount of connective tissue which will cause roast to be tough if not cooked thoroughly.

When cooking veal in liquid or by braising, test for tenderness by piercing with fork. Continue cooking until meat is tender to the fork touch.

Timetable for roasting veal.

Cut of meat	Ready-to-cook weight	Approximate roasting time at 325° F.	Internal temperature of meat when done
	Pounds	*Hours*	° *F.*
Leg...............	5 to 8	2 1/2 to 3 1/2	170
Loin..............	5	3	170
Shoulder..........	6	3 1/2	170

Timetable for braising veal.

Cut of meat	Approximate ready-to-cook weight or thickness	Approximate total cooking time
		Hours
Chops................	1/2 to 3/4 inch........	3/4
Shoulder, rolled.......	3 to 5 pounds..........	2 to 2 1/2

Veal cutlets are one-half inch thick slices usually cut from the leg.

To pound paper-thin for scaloppine, place slice between two pieces of waxed paper and pound with a mallet. If you don't own a mallet, the bottom of a heavy skillet will do very nicely.

One pound of veal cutlets will normally serve three.

Ground veal is tastier when combined with ground ham as veal alone is too dry. This combination makes delicious veal patties.

Poultry seasoning is excellent for improving the flavor of veal.

VEGETABLES: Properly cooked vegetables are attractive and colorful.

Vegetables are rich with vitamins and minerals but overcooking lowers both eating quality and nutritive value. Therefore, cook vegetables quickly, with little or no water, and serve as soon as possible.

Never wash before refrigeration since washing increases the chance of spoilage. Therefore, wash just before cooking or eating.

To preserve freshness, produce should be wrapped tightly in plastic bags before refrigeration.

To prevent vitamin loss, salt vegetables *after* cooking.

Simmering vegetables in milk stabilizes color and tenderizes faster than water.

To restore sweetness to overmature vegetables, add a teaspoon of sugar to the cooking water.

To heat canned vegetables properly, drain liquid from the can into a saucepan. Boil the liquid first and then add the vegetables for quick heating. Texture and shape will be undisturbed.

All leftover liquid from cooking vegetables should be saved and used in cooking soups or gravies. This liquid contains many minerals and vitamins.

Vegetable	Boiling time (Minutes)	Vegetable	Boiling time (Minutes)
Asparagus, whole	10 to 13	Okra	12 to 14
Beans:		Onions, mature:	
Lima	25 to 27	Whole	11 to 15
Snap, 1-inch pieces	13 to 15	Quartered	10 to 14
Beets, whole	38 to 40	Parsnips:	
Broccoli, heavy stalks,		Whole	20 to 40
split	9 to 12	Quartered	8 to 15
Brussels sprouts	15 to 17	Peas	10 to 14
Cabbage:		Potatoes	
Shredded	6 to 8	Whole, medium size	25 to 29
Wedges	10 to 13	Quartered	15 to 17
Carrots:		Spinach	8 to 12
Whole	20 to 22	Squash	
Sliced or diced	18 to 20	Acorn, quartered	18 to 20
Cauliflower:		Butternut, cubed	16 to 18
Separated	8 to 12	Yellow, crookneck,	
Whole	20 to 24	sliced	11 to 13
Celery, sliced	15 to 19	Zucchini, sliced	13 to 15
Collards	15 to 20	Sweetpotatoes, whole	28 to 35
Corn:		Turnips:	
On cob	5 to 7	Cut up	10 to 12
Whole kernel	6 to 8	Whole	30 to 38
Kale	15 to 20		

For an unusual centerpiece, switch from flowers to fresh vegetables. Try surrounding a glossy black eggplant with bunches of carrots, radishes, etc.

VICHYSSOISE: A very rich cold leek and potato cream soup.

VINAIGRETTE: A sauce made from a mixture of oil, vinegar, salt, ground pepper and occasionally herbs.

WAFFLES: To test heat of waffle iron, sprinkle a few drops of water on it. If water boils and forms a ball, it is ready. If water sizzles violently, iron is too hot.

For best results, fill waffle iron two-thirds full.

Store leftover batter in covered container in refrigerator. Before using again, add one teaspoon baking powder which has been dissolved in one tablespoon milk for each cup of batter.

WALNUTS: One pound in shell yields one-half pound shelled.

One pound shelled walnuts yields 4 1/2 cups.

For a fast and tasty hors d'oeuvre, sandwich any firm cheese dip between two walnut halves.

See also **NUTS.**

WATERCRESS: A peppery-tasting salad green that grows in fresh water.

To keep fresh and crisp, wash thoroughly, shake off excess water and refrigerate in glass-covered jar.

See also **SALAD.**

WATER ICE: A frozen dessert made of fruit juice or puree with the addition of water and other ingredients.

WATERMELON: Select ripe watermelon with a somewhat dull surface and a creamy color underneath. Interior should be fully red and firm with mature black seeds.

Watermelon is always best served iced cold.

For a change of pace, try a watermelon drink. Cut small pieces, remove seeds, and whirl in blender. Pour over ice cubes.

WHIP: To increase the volume of a liquid and make it frothy by beating air into it.

WHIPPED CREAM: For more successful whipping, chill cream, bowl and rotary beaters for two hours before starting.

Cream doubles in bulk when whipped.

Always whip at medium speed.

To correct whipped cream that has been overwhipped and is therefore somewhat buttery, gently whip in one to two tablespoons of light cream or undiluted evaporated milk.

WHISK: A kitchen utensil for rapidly whipping eggs, cream, puddings, etc.

WINE: Wine works magic with food. Its bewitching flavor can camouflage leftovers, enhance soups and turn the most ordinary dish into a gourmet's delight.

Wine adds a festive touch to a meal and the colorful bottles add atmosphere to any dinner table.

As a rule of thumb, serve white wines with chicken and fish; red wines with beef, pork, game and cheese but more about this later.

Wine bottles should be stored on their sides so that the corks are kept in touch with the liquid. When corks dry out they shrink and permit air in which spoils the wine.

Stored bottles should periodically be moved gently so that any sediment in the bottom is undisturbed.

Chill white or rosé wines in the refrigerator for several hours before serving.

Serve red wines at room temperature, about 65 degrees.

Sparkling wines deteriorate if they are cooled and not used. Avoid double cooling.

If more than one wine is to be served at a meal remember that a drier wine precedes a sweet one and a lighter wine comes before a heavy one.

Before a meal try dry sherry or chilled sweet vermouth with a twist of lemon.

Avoid serving red wines with shellfish. This combination causes a metallic taste to many fish eaters. Try a dry white wine such as chablis, sancerre and muscadot.

Grilled or poached fish go well with sweet wines such as meursault, montrachot or rhine wines.

Port is favored at the close of a hearty meal with cheese, walnuts or fruit.

Serve a sweet wine with dessert or between meals.

Serve champagne for any occasion, throughout a meal or with dessert.

Store unused portion of white and red wines in refrigerator. If kept for more than a few days, use in cooking.

Dessert wines may be opened and kept for a much longer period of time.

Wines that have turned sour may be used in salad dressings or tart sauces.

When cooking with red wines, add a few slices of raw carrots to cut the tartness.

Never drink wine with curry (try beer instead).

For added zest, try one tablespoon of muscatel added to mincemeat.

WINE GLASSES: There are many types available, some of which are:

2-3 ounce size for appetizers.
4-6 ounce size for table wines.
Hollow stem or *tulip* for champagne and sparkling wines.

Clear untinted glass is preferable to colored glass as it permits the natural color of the wine to sparkle through.

At a table setting, the wine glasses are placed to the right, just a little below the water glass.

Glasses are left on table for filling, not lifted, and should properly be about three-quarters full.

YAM: Select firm, smooth and clean yams or sweet potatoes. Damp or soft spots may indicate decay.

Six medium-sized yams yield about two cups mashed.

Puncture one end to prevent bursting during baking.

For crisp skin when baking, first grease with a little shortening.

YEAST: To test compressed yeast for freshness, crumble into water. If it breaks clean, it is fresh. If it becomes mushy, yeast is old.

for successful dissolving:
Compressed—dissolve in lukewarm water or milk at 80° to 90° F.
Active Dry—dissolve in warmer water at 110° to 115° F. Never dissolve active dry yeast in milk.

For successful rising, always scald milk first and then cool to lukewarm before adding compressed yeast.

To test yeast dough, press two fingers into the dough. If the depression made by fingers fills quickly, the dough is not ready. If holes remain, it has risen enough.

YOGURT: Made from partly evaporated and fermented milk.

To save calories, use yogurt instead of sour cream for salad dressing.

Make your own frozen pops by mixing yogurt with nuts and chocolate chips. Freeze in paper baking cups with wooden sticks inserted in center. When frozen, peel off paper and voila!

ZABAGLIONE: A dessert made from eggs, sugar and wine beaten over boiling water until thick. Served either warm or cold in dessert or parfait glasses.

Occasionally used as a sauce for fruit.

ZEPPOLE: An Italian doughnut-like pastry fried plain or filled with foods.

ZUCCHINI: Select small and narrow zucchini which are heavy for their size with tender rinds and a glossy appearance.

See also **SQUASH and VEGETABLES.**